Jan Kern's *Seduced by Sex : Saved by Love—A Journey Out of False Intimacy* is an engaging, warm, disturbing, and powerful look at the journey from brokenness to healing. With compelling tenderness, Jan writes about the harsh realities of the pain and heartache of sexual experience outside of God's design, and does so without being preachy or shallow. This book is real, and important. Offering hope to those who are in the midst of sexual wandering and confusion, and a wake-up call to those dabbling on the edges, *Seduced by Sex : Saved by Love* is a gift of grace.

—Chap Clark, senior editor, *YouthWorker Journal*;
author, *Hurt: Inside the World of Today's Teenagers*

It's refreshing to read a book for teens on the issue of sex that is not only frank, but also compassionate and insightful. Jan doesn't try to fix teens, but instead, through the power of story, shows that there are other options. She offers choices that are empowering and life-changing.

—T. Suzanne Eller, international speaker and author;
founder, Real Teen Faith ministries

Having sex before you're married is one of the biggest lies of the world. I once chose to believe it, and then I became a Christian and discovered that God has a different plan for my life. But when I started reading this book, I realized I hadn't fully dealt with my past and still needed healing. Jan's book has helped me look at the lies and my past and find truth, peace, and love from God himself. *Seduced by Sex : Saved by Love* changed my life.

—Sherry H., age 19, student

Seduced by Sex : Saved by Love is powerful, convicting, and raw! It spoke so much truth into my own life, and it is one of those books you just can't put down. Its story-style testimonies are so powerful and real they made me take a deeper look into my own life and the standards I set for myself concerning sex and purity. The book is a must read. . . . The outcome from reading it is walking out of darkness and into truth and light, and it is backed by God's Word told in ways young adults like myself can relate to.

—Ricky Chenoweth, age 20, college student

In *Seduced by Sex : Saved by Love—A Journey Out of False Intimacy*, Jan takes a raw and honest look at the angst of adolescence that's rarely seen in Christian books for teenagers. Not only does she delve into the core issues, she offers practical hope that will connect with this generation of students.

—Ginny Olson, author, *Teenage Girls:
Exploring Issues Adolescent Girls Face and Strategies to Help Them*

Seduced by Sex : Saved by Love is a must read for every teen, youth worker, and parent. This compelling personal story mixed with compassionate insight and thoughtful personal application has something for all of us. Whether you're struggling with the seductive lies of the world, the desire to fit in, or watching friends make painful decisions and want to help, you'll find a wealth of wisdom here.

—Pam Stenzel, author, *Sex Has a Price Tag:
Discussions About Sensuality, Spirituality, and Self Respect*

With this book, Jan peers into the hearts of teenagers and young adults and exposes the lies that they—that all of us—are prone to believe. She displays an uncanny insight into how so many are slowly seduced into a lifestyle that strips them of their innocence and hope for meaningful love. This book helps unwrap the mystery of recovering from these lies and builds hope into the lives of its readers.

—Garth Heckman, author, *Burn This Book: Ignite a New Life with God*

Jan has entered deeply into topics most worthy of exploration: the longing of one's soul to be authentically accepted and loved, and the fear of never finding those things. In *Seduced by Sex : Saved by Love*, she clearly shows that desperate people do desperate things, but that there also is a way through and out of the entrapments of this generation's overly sexualized culture. There is hope to be found in Suzy's story—a promise for fulfillment that ends, as it was intended to be in her beginning, with God's design and imprint on her very human heart.

—Susan Hicks, marriage and family therapist,
Christian Encounter Ministries

Suzy's courageous story richly illustrates her journey from brokenness into restoration and celebration of what God intended for her best. Jan Kern pulls back the curtain and reveals, through story, the truth behind today's experiences of love and sexuality, illustrating what we often experience when making our own choices—betrayal, heartache, disillusionment, and despair. She offers biblical guidelines and a fresh look into the loving heart of our creator, who forgives us and wants to heal us in our brokenness. In this book I feel I've found a tool of hope to share with teens and young adults who need a bridge to God's heart from the wreckage of their sexual pasts.

—Linda Carlos, marriage and family therapist, Elk Grove, California

SEDUCED BY SEX : SAVED BY LOVE

A JOURNEY OUT OF FALSE INTIMACY // JAN KERN

A LIVE FREE BOOK

SEDUCED BY SEX : SAVED BY LOVE

Standard®
PUBLISHING
Bringing The Word to Life

Cincinnati, Ohio

Published by Standard Publishing, Cincinnati, Ohio
www.standardpub.com

Printed in the United States of America

Project editor: Robert Irvin
Cover design: Studio Gearbox
Interior design: Edward Willis Group, Inc.

Cover photograph by Tara Wallace

Published in association with the Books & Such Literary Agency, 52 Mission Circle, Suite 122, PMB 170, Santa Rosa, CA 95409-5370, www.booksandsuch.biz.

ISBN 978-0-7847-2158-2

Library of Congress Cataloging-in-Publication Data

Kern, Jan, 1956-
  Seduced by sex, saved by love : a journey out of false intimacy / Jan Kern.
     p. cm.
  ISBN 978-0-7847-2158-2 (perfect bound)
  1. Sex instruction for teenagers--United States. 2. Sex instruction for teenagers--Religious aspects--Christianity. 3. Christian teenagers--Religious life. 4. Sex in mass media. 5. Mass media and sex--United States. I. Title.

HQ35.K464 2008
241.66--dc22

2007039728

14 13 12 11 10 09 08   9 8 7 6 5 4 3 2 1

DEDICATION

To the CEM students . . .

Thank you for showing me what it means to powerfully live out Christ's transforming love. When you really "get it," there's no stopping you.

Keep living free.

CONTENTS

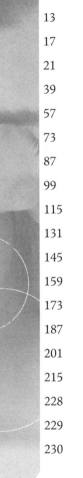

'I WAS SEDUCED . . . '

I WAS SEDUCED BY SEX.

I didn't know it then, but I'm painfully aware of it now.

I wish I could have learned from someone else's mistakes, but being stubborn, I chose to suffer from my own failures. Unfortunately, the consequences with sex aren't the same as when you don't study well enough for your SATs and miss out on your preferred college. Or mess up at school and get kicked out—jeopardizing your diploma. Or injure yourself taking that sweet jump at the skateboard park, ruining your chance for a football scholarship.

Although serious enough, none of these compare to the impact sex can have on our lives outside of marriage. Satan is a scheming, condemning liar. He tantalizes us with sex before marriage, making it appear as normal stuff, harmless fun. Yet when we give in to his schemes, he'll spend the rest of our lives working to condemn us because we gave in.

That's what he did to me—or tried to. For twenty-five years—what could have been some of the best years of my life— I let him torment me with shame and regret. And that weight harmed all my relationships—with God, with my husband, with my children, and with my friends. Yet I didn't know why. Now I do. And so I share it with you—because I'd rather you learn from my mistakes than suffer through your own.

God has taught me a lot on my journey, including two very compelling lessons. First, sex before marriage is not the same as sex inside of marriage. That's what all the messages out there try to convince us of—that it's just as good, it's just as exciting—

but it's simply not true. Sex outside of marriage is pretty much opposite of what God planned for sex when shared within marriage. And the truth is that sex outside of marriage has great power to ruin sex inside of marriage.

Not only is it *not* the same sex, it will keep you from having the kind of passionate, wild sex that God has planned for you within a marriage. Struggling to believe this? I know it's hard to imagine right now, when you're not married. But I know this is true because it happened to me. And I'm not alone. Now that God uses my mess to help other people, I hear my story repeated over and over by others who have traveled a similar path. God wants you to have great sex in marriage—Satan doesn't. It's as simple as that.

The second lesson God has taught me is that although sex isn't worse than other sins, it is different. Yes, God can forgive all sin—even sexual sin. But in 1 Corinthians 6:18, he spells it out clearly: All other sins are committed outside the body, but sex is the only sin that we commit against *ourselves*.

Although forgiveness is an essential component with sexual sin, it's not the only one. The other necessary piece of our journey to wholeness is healing. Sex isn't just a physical act; it involves the spirit, soul, and emotions. I give *all* of myself to someone else. And outside of marriage that means I wound all of myself and all of someone else. I'm not talking about a nasty bruise that lasts a couple of weeks. The wounds from sex can linger for a lifetime.

If you let them. I could have, but I didn't.

God uses healing, along with forgiveness, to restore us to wholeness—physically, emotionally, and spiritually. It's a miracle, I know, but God is the master of miracles.

For me, reading this book was like reading my story . . . except it's a story that belongs to another. Putting the messages of this book into practice might save your future marriage. Doing the same could even save your life.

I was seduced by sex . . . but saved by love—God's amazing love.

—Barbara Wilson, author, *The Invisible Bond:*
How to Break Free from Your Sexual Past

GETTING THE DIALOGUE GOING . . .

SEX. What a *huge* topic.

Let's talk about it. Yes, openly. And maybe somewhat differently than you have before.

Let's look at it through the true story of Suzy, whose search for acceptance and belonging led her into the arms of false intimacy. Yet hers *is* a love story—one of God pursuing her in her weariness and pain. One in which God helped her discover the amazing power of true intimacy.

But let's look at sex through the stories of others too—because each of our encounters in grappling with the ideas and experiences in our sexuality is unique.

Let's talk about the crazy, distorted version of sex that is in our faces every day, and how we can regain and hold on to a truer picture of what it's really all about.

Most of all, let's bring it to the level of the heart—a heart that matters and can't be ignored when it comes to sex. A heart that is extremely important to God, your creator—*yours*.

Your heart may be confused, broken, or even hardened through your own experiences with false intimacy—a kind of intimacy that counterfeits the sex you were designed by God to enjoy. The questions, the misconceptions, the pain, just the topic itself might feel so overwhelming that it's difficult to think of facing it . . . or facing yourself.

If it is difficult, I encourage you to find a person (of your gender) who can read through this book with you. A parent, friend, youth leader, pastor, or mentor—someone who has wisdom in this area and solidly knows God's true design for sex. One moment at a time, one choice at a time—you can begin to find healing and wholeness again.

Due to the extremely personal nature of this topic, Suzy and I have chosen to be sensitive to the identities of others in her story. The names of many of her friends and the young men in her life have been changed; so has the name of her high school. In addition, for privacy, the names of others who have graciously and authentically shared their stories were changed.

Also, in light of the personal nature of this topic, I think of you, the reader. Maybe you're just not sure what to think about sex—what's right and wrong, what's the proper context. And what God's design, purposes, and timing for its full enjoyment are all about. Even if you're feeling like you've heard all this before, I encourage you to join in, to continue the dialogue. Prayer is a great place to start. Here's one to use if you'd like:

> *This is a big topic, God. I bring all of my thoughts, feelings, and questions to you. I bring you all of my experiences—including the times when I've chosen something outside of your design for me in the area of sex. As I'm taking steps to really grab hold of your plan for me in my life and relationships, help me begin to see the snares that can lead me into false intimacy. Help me, Lord, to catch a glimpse of where you want to take me with all of this, of what true intimacy is about according to you. Help me long for that. Amen.*

I pray for a journey of amazing discovery for you.

Jan

one

I wanted people to see me differently. I wanted to be the bad girl.
It was my way of taking my life in my hands.
I was in control, running the show.

THE BELL RANG. Suzy clicked her pen, closed her spiral notebook, and slid it with her math book into her book bag. As she stood, she tugged her short, blue skirt and pulled her bag over her shoulder.

"Hey, Suzy. I've seen you around with Matt. What's up with that?" One of the guys in the class wanted to know.

Suzy felt warmth creep across her face. "Yeah, he's my boyfriend." She could hardly believe it herself. Matt was one of the popular guys in tenth grade. He also had a bad boy reputation, but she didn't mind. It went with the new image she was creating for herself.

To avoid further questions, she hurried to step in with the crowd squeezing through the door and spilling onto the outdoor walkway. Partway down, several of her friends had gathered, and she turned to join them. Danny, a guy she'd known since junior high, was with them, and he lifted his head in a nod as she approached. Lately he had been giving her the attention she had sought from him . . . for what seemed like forever. She stepped into a space in their circle and listened to their talk about what they were doing for lunch. She felt Danny's glances. It was nice. They had been friends. Maybe they could be more, if it wasn't for—

Smack.

Matt had walked up, laid a loud kiss on Suzy's lips, then spun away toward his friends. Still moving, he called back to her. "Hey, when you get home from school call me, OK? We can meet up." With a quick raise of his eyebrows, he grinned.

> **She felt Danny's glances. It was nice. They had been friends. Maybe they could be more, if it wasn't for—**

"OK." Suzy smiled. As Matt walked away, she caught Danny watching her. He seemed hurt. *Why does Danny have to like me now?*, she thought to herself. She looked back to watch Matt jabbing his friends and laughing before he turned a corner and was out of sight.

Yeah, Matt was cute.

And popular.

She liked those two things, a lot—even if she didn't know much else about him at all.

At home, after school, Suzy dropped her book bag on her bed. She turned and faced her reflection. The brown-framed, full-length mirror leaned against the wall next to her closet. She retucked her shirt, then pulled it until it accented her small waist just right. She smiled.

A few months ago I was a no-name. I don't have to be one of those anymore.

She picked up her hairbrush and ran it through her long, brown hair. With her fingers she adjusted her bangs while at the same time checking her makeup. Some of the mascara and eyeliner had smudged during the day, so she hunted through her makeup case for a tissue to fix it. When she finished, she turned, slowly, for an all-over inspection.

"Oh." She spun back around, rummaged through the case again, added fresh lip-gloss, and then straightened. "There."

She stared at her reflection, then began to reason aloud with herself. "Do you really want to call Matt? You know what he wants to do today." She waited, but didn't expect an argument from the girl staring back at her—someone she was beginning not to recognize. And that was due to more than the extra makeup.

> **She turned and faced her reflection.**
> **She retucked her shirt, then pulled it until**
> **it accented her small waist just right.**
> **She smiled.**

Finally, she tossed her head as if to shake off the doubts. *I know what I want. I've got Matt. This is my chance to really break into that new image. Drop the goody-goody stuff.*

Suzy turned from the mirror, picked up her phone, and punched in Matt's number.

"Hi, it's Suzy."

"Hey."

"So where do you want to meet?"

"Come over to my house." He paused. "No one will be home for hours."

"OK, I'll walk over. I'll be there soon."

They hung up, and Suzy glanced once more in the mirror. Her heart beat fast. *Stop thinking so much. It's not such a hard choice. I've got a lot to gain, right?*

"Do you really want to call Matt? You know what he wants to do today." She waited, but didn't expect an argument.

Cars whizzed past as Suzy stepped onto the sidewalk along a street that dissected some area neighborhoods. She thought about a discipleship meeting with some of the girls at a Christian club for high schoolers that she attended recently. "It's God's plan for you to save sex for marriage" was the message that night. She'd heard that a zillion times, but what was the big deal? Several of her friends had done it. Why should she be left out?

Suzy slowed her walk as she recalled the talk one of the guys gave about the whole relationship concept—what love really is, and isn't.

She and Matt had only been dating a short time. *Dating? Right.* They'd connected at the mall when she offered him a cigarette. Since then, they'd only talked a few times, walked to some classes together. *I know this isn't love. I know. But I'm just starting to feel accepted by the popular kids. Matt as my boyfriend guarantees it.*

　　　　　　　　SEDUCED BY SEX : SAVED BY LOVE

She was only halfway aware of the truck tires slowing and crunching the pavement nearby, but she kept walking, lost in thought.

"Suzy!"

She turned and saw Justin, an older friend she knew from her youth club. He pulled his truck to a stop, then leaned toward the window on the side where Suzy had been walking. "My dog is hurt. Can you help?"

She could see Justin was shaken. "Oh, that's awful." Suzy peered through the open window and saw the black pup lying on the seat, wrapped in Justin's jacket. It was whimpering and wriggling in pain. "What happened?" She jerked the door open.

"He got hit by a car."

Suzy slid partway onto the seat and gently stroked the dog's side. "Ohhh—he's really hurt."

"Yeah, I've got to do something fast." The dog tried to get up and Justin settled him back down. "Can you help me get him to a vet?"

> ## *Stop thinking so much. It's not such a hard choice. I've got a lot to gain, right?*

"I, uh . . . I'm on my way over to . . . I . . . I've got something to do." She couldn't look at Justin. Shouldn't she help? The old Suzy would have. Her stomach clenched as she wrestled with this choice.

Justin reached over and adjusted the jacket around the

restless dog. "I don't think he's going to hold still."

Suzy edged back toward the door. "I'm sorry. I really can't go with you." Her thoughts, though, were tugging at her—hard. *I should. Besides, this could totally be my way out of . . .*

"It's all right." Justin shifted anxiously in his seat. "I better get going."

> **She thought about a guy she knew and what he had said to her earlier that day. He seemed to be watching her and, when she turned to him, he said, "You've changed."**

"Yeah." Suzy slid out of the truck and shut the door. She watched Justin drive away; she felt awful. *Matt couldn't get mad about not showing up if I was helping a friend . . .*

"It doesn't matter," she argued with herself, aloud. "Justin won't care tomorrow, but I'll care if I don't get to Matt's."

She crossed the busy street, followed it past a pond, then entered Matt's neighborhood. She'd soon be at his house.

As she turned a corner, she thought about a guy she knew and what he had said to her earlier that day. She had walked into science class and sat down. He seemed to be watching her and, when she turned to him, he said, "You've changed." She knew what he meant.

She thought back to the serious expression on his face. *He said I've changed? Well, that's only the point.*

Still, her stomach tightened in some kind of warning.

A couple of streets, a couple of bends, and she spotted Matt

SEDUCED BY SEX : SAVED BY LOVE

outside his friend's house on a corner. He saw her too.

"Hey."

"Hi, Matt."

Matt walked over and put his arm around Suzy's waist.

"So what are you guys up to?" Josh's voice had that mocking edge to it.

"We're going to my house to watch porn," Matt said over his shoulder, giving it right back to his friend.

"Yeah, right."

Suzy tensed. Questions and cautions spun through her mind, but she fought to push them away. She swallowed. She was there. She'd stay.

Matt pulled her closer and smiled at her, his eyes half closed. She tried to look deeper into those eyes. What *did* he feel for her? If she went through with this, would he like her more?

> **Is this supposed to be Matt's bedroom, or is it just for—?**

His house was just a few down the street from Josh's. They went in the side door of the garage. A bed was off to one corner. It sat among boxes, coolers, and bicycles.

Is this supposed to be Matt's bedroom, or is it just for—?

"So, do you want to do this?" Matt let go of Suzy and took a step toward the bed.

She knew what he meant, even though they had never talked about it. "Yeah . . . I guess." She felt her heart racing. She had never had sex. *What's going to happen?* Guilt edged in around the fringes of her nerves.

What are you doing, *Suzy? It shouldn't be like this—a dirty garage, someone you hardly know. It should mean so much more.* One moment she felt the wrongness of it all. The next it was like nothing.

Like a person losing their hold on the edge of a cliff as each finger loses its grip, Suzy's struggling emotions began to detach and fall away. This moment was right for now—she didn't want to think beyond it. And then one last thought quivered on the edge before it too fell away . . .

God, I hope your grace will be there when I decide to clean up my life.

Matt's voice broke through her thoughts. "Suzy?"

She looked up and caught his annoyed frown. "What?"

"I said, Got any problem if I use a condom?"

"No." *Of course not.* That much she knew from the sex talks.

> ## God, I hope your grace will be there when I decide to clean up my life.

The force of her resolve shattered all other cautions. This was the *only* way to gain the acceptance she hoped for. She would do what it took to get it.

As Matt pulled her into his arms and onto the bed, she fully gave in to this goal.

In the next several moments she felt a faint but deep twinge in her heart. Like the sad dying of something important.

> You've kept track of my every toss
> and turn through the sleepless nights,
> Each tear entered in your ledger,
> each ache written in your book.
>
> PSALM 56:8 (THE MESSAGE)

ACCEPTANCE AT A COST

A new image. Like putting on a different jacket.

That's how Suzy viewed her quest to be noticed, to be accepted, the way she desired at school. Looking back to that time, she says, "I knew exactly what I was doing. I knew all the 'Christian' things that I should have and shouldn't have done, but I wanted to be identified with the crowd that did things wrong." Suzy was convinced that Matt saw her as nothing more than another conquest, so why should she see him as anything more than a stepping-stone to further break into the new image she was building?

Nothing would derail her. Not even a friend who needed help with his badly injured dog. Suzy remembers that representative moment with regret. "I had been the kind of person who would help in a situation like that," she said. "But I was so far gone at that point."

Also wrapped up in that moment was Suzy's fading desire to respond to God's warnings. And she recognized it. When Justin drove up and stopped her in her tracks, she realized she had an unmistakable opportunity to make a different choice.

"God totally gave me an out," she recalled. "It's a painting of that Bible verse—when you are tempted he'll give a way to escape."

It's in 1 Corinthians 10:13 that God, through the writer, Paul, talks about providing a means to escape from sin. But Suzy chose not to escape. She went to Matt's place knowing what they were going to do—and how little it meant to either of them. "Looking back, I can't believe I was so flippant with that decision," she said.

How did Suzy reach that point? In the next few chapters, we'll go back to the events that led to her decision to go to Matt's. The rest of the book follows her story and what happened after that day.

Even today it's difficult for Suzy to identify the source of the deeper conflicts and pain that rooted her so solidly on such a focused and self-destructive path. She was driven by a need for acceptance, a desire to belong. Sex was a tool, nothing more—a perspective she believes she picked up from TV and the movies. *No big deal. Do it. Move on.*

She had only a faint sense of how her actions would impact the rest of her life. "I was thinking God would forgive me later. Here I am, on the other side, forgiven, but when you choose to give yourself away to somebody, you don't ever, ever, ever get that back. It has forever changed my life and will forever affect me."

Sex.

No big deal?

Each of us can have a huge impact on how someone else views and values relationships—and what can come from those relationships, up to and including sex. Pray about getting your own perspective in line with God's design. And then watch for appropriate times to have open and sensitive conversations.

It's So Much More

Popular beliefs and values about sex have become sadly twisted—this gift from God has been spun far from the original purpose and design he had in mind. Mix that with a push to fit in and it's easy to be lured by the temptation. That's why so many—Suzy, maybe you—have been enticed by the attraction of casual sex.

Others have their stories of why they chased sex, what they believed it would do for them.

Ryan was sixteen when he began his sexual activity. "I grew up thinking that sex really had nothing to do with marriage," he said. "If you asked me if I thought of sex as sacred, I would have looked at you with a big question mark on my face. That God gave us the gift of sex for marriage wasn't even a thought in my mind. So I believed if I got laid—as some of my family and friends put it—I went up a step in being a man."

As he looked back, he remembered feeling there must be something more. "A better way? A better person? A better age? When sex outside of marriage happens there is so much guilt, regret, and so many questions. It's not worth it." Looking to the future, Ryan says, "There will be a time when it's right, and I'll be with the one God has for me. Then there'll be nothing better."

Nicole had been dating her boyfriend for a couple of years. At seventeen she had sex with him because she believed that "giving my body equaled getting love in return." She adds, "I was hungry for attention and love, and I was so afraid that he would leave me if I didn't give in."

First time, and she got pregnant. Then she secretly had an abortion.

"I had this facade. I was the all-American girl," Nicole said. She was involved in sports, did well in her honors courses, and was voted the prom queen. "And everyone thought I was a pure, proper virgin."

Like Ryan, she now believes that not waiting for the right time for sex is the wrong decision. "One choice can take you down a course of destruction. I am getting back on my feet, but it has taken so much heartache and time to get here." She prays that she can help others avoid similar mistakes and feels strongly that true intimacy is worth the wait.

Look again at the beliefs behind the choices that brought only disappointment, heartache, and shame:

Suzy was sure that changing her image, which included having sex, would add up to the acceptance and popularity she craved.

Nicole believed she would feel loved and wouldn't be alone.

Ryan was told sex would make him a man.

Each person felt a need that seemed very real at the time. We're created to operate on love, acceptance, and the expression of all God made us to be, including through our sexuality. And it's true that an intimate sexual relationship between two people can encompass those elements and more. But heartache and disillusionment also enter when the timing and circumstances are off track.

Sex was God's idea—not man's. God designed it in such a way that it is disappointing, even destructive, if done out of sync with his plan. It becomes false intimacy—like taking a precious gift, greedily opening it before the right time, and then using it for all the wrong purposes and in ways it was never meant to be used. Or even giving the gift away—believing that the one who is asking for it *now* is the one who is meant to open it. But then someone else asks for it too, and someone else . . .

True intimacy is an amazing gift from God. It's designed to be shared exclusively between a man and a woman—who are bound together in marriage—for life. It's something extremely unique and special. "Sacred," to use Ryan's word.

In the meantime, what do you do with your longing for acceptance? For fitting in or being loved or valued? Those things are important. You are important—enough to consider your choices carefully.

You don't have to go it alone. God is in this with you.

Look around. You probably know someone who needs to feel they are loved and accepted, that they belong. If those things are missing, that person could be in danger of heading toward self-destructive choices, including risky sexual behavior. Talk. Invite. Connect. Show you care.

I WANT

Can you imagine having the love of someone who is so familiar with who you are that before you speak that person knows exactly what you need? Someone who cares so deeply about you that he would never hurt you or want harm to come to you? Who wants the very best for you in every possible way, and will do anything to make sure that happens?

"The Lord is my shepherd, I shall not . . . want" (Psalm 23:1).

This comes straight out of a sacred song written by David, once a shepherd himself, thousands of years ago. It's possible he was a teen at the time he wrote it; if not, no doubt he was thinking back to that time in his life. You may have heard this particular verse many times—though maybe not in the context of sex and relationships.

Picture the shepherd who David writes about. He's devoted to caring for his sheep, determined to guide them into pastures where there will be safety and richness and where they can run free. If one strays, he brings it back. He shows his sheep how to follow the paths of "rightness" that keep them on track and lead to more rich pastures. The sheep that stay close to him experience his comfort, abundance, goodness, faithful love, and presence—every day of their lives. The shepherd loves them completely and would do anything for them. A sheep under the care of this kind of shepherd isn't lacking for anything.

Jesus *is* that kind of shepherd. And in his presence "I shall not want."

Want what? What others might have that's not healthy for my mind, body, spirit. Love—the wrong kind of love—that I might find myself longing for and "needing" *now*. My desires satisfied . . . at any cost—*now*.

Want grabs hold of my mind and doesn't let go. It creates desires so overpowering that I no longer believe or even remember that my shepherd has my best interest in mind. *Want* deceives. It tempts. It says: "You need it and you should have it now."

A response that won't leave us with deep feelings of guilt, shame, and a lack of true fulfillment?

I'll wait for my shepherd. He knows the right stage of life for this experience.

You may have needs and longings that have driven you to crazy places, including into the arms of false intimacy— that place where you let go of God's amazing design and gift and accept the counterfeit. You may have stepped into sexual choices that have a hold on your mind and heart in ways no one understands.

Except God—he knows. He aches over you when he sees you struggling or trying to fulfill your needs and desires in ways that will only hurt you and others. He knows there's something better for you. Freedom within his rich pastures. Safety. His guidance as your shepherd.

Do you trust him with your deepest needs? Ask him, or ask others who know him well, to help you see his guidance and his boundaries as a way to bring true freedom into your life. And, in the case of sex, he can bring you true, rich, and full intimacy as it was designed. Not *now*, but at the right time. And in the best way—in the beauty and wonder in which it was designed.

God can be your shepherd. And when he is, you'll find that you lack nothing.

God, sometimes the needs and longings I feel are so strong, I don't know what to do with them. Help me to see you as my shepherd, someone who loves me beyond anything I can imagine and who knows my deepest needs more than I do. Show me when I'm beginning to follow a path that can only hurt me or others. I want to trust you and understand more fully your design for relationships. While I'm still learning, help me when I am tempted. Give me the strength to wait for the fullness of the rich pastures you have in mind for me. AMEN.

As a shepherd looks after his scattered flock
when he is with them, so will I look after my sheep.
I will rescue them from all the places where they were
scattered on a day of clouds and darkness.

EZEKIEL 34:12

GOING DEEPER

- Think about what you might be hungering for in friendships and family relationships. How might you be in danger of compromising your values to meet those needs?

- What beliefs about love and acceptance do you operate from? Think carefully about your past. In what ways can these beliefs be adjusted to more accurately fit with the way God sees you?

- Beginning to see ourselves as God sees us is a good first step in honoring God's design for our lives. What specific steps can you take to help yourself wait for his timing in your life?

DEEPER STILL

Use a journal or notebook to begin to write letters to God, your true shepherd. Tell him honestly about your desires and struggles. After you write the first letter, think of Psalm 23 and what God might write back to you as encouragement.

two

*Whatever wave would come in, and what people were doing or saying,
that's what I could become. Totally fake.
Totally creating a foundation for losing myself.*

GOING BACK TO THE BEGINNING . . .

Suzy stared out the car window; she pressed her arm against her stomach. It rumbled. Hunger? Nerves? Probably both.

Her gaze absently followed the string of restaurants, coffee shops, and shopping centers that lined the busy street leading to her high school. Her focus landed on a guy walking down the street. *Nice-looking* guy. He turned her way as they passed, nodded, smiled, and kept watching her.

Her breath caught as she leaned back against her seat. She slid a glance to Mom, who was focused on maneuvering the car through the congested traffic. She squelched her smile, but excitement flushed her cheeks. *This could work. I could pull this off.*

That morning she had woken extra early. It didn't matter that today was only orientation and class sign-ups. She had primed all summer for this—trying out makeup, hairstyles, and different outfits with her friends. Today, as she got ready, she saw the transformation. She knew she wasn't the same plain girl who had tumbled out of bed in baggy pajama bottoms and a T-shirt. Now her hair hung just right and a couple of tweaks with the curling iron put her bangs at the angle she wanted. Her makeup went on exactly as she had practiced. She felt great in the loaned white shorts and black, cropped top that showed off her slim figure and newly acquired curves.

Would friends who hadn't seen her all summer notice the change?

> **Today, as she got ready, she saw the transformation. She knew she wasn't the same plain girl who had tumbled out of bed in baggy pajama bottoms and a T-shirt. Now her hair hung just right.**

Mom pulled the car into the parking lot and angled it into a space, then kept it idling. "You'll catch a ride home?"

"Yeah, no problem. See ya, Mom." Suzy slid out and shut the car door, then straightened and pulled the back of her shorts. As she started up the path already filling with students, she scanned the crowd for Kaela. When she spotted her she wove her way through the crowd until she was by Kaela's side.

Kaela turned as she came up. "Jenn's shorts, my top—it works. You look great."

"Thanks. You too." Suzy smiled at her friend, a couple of inches shorter, soft red hair. Kaela could pull off any outfit.

"I guess we're supposed to find our line over by the cafeteria to get our class schedule." Kaela squeezed Suzy's arm in excitement. "Can you believe we're finally starting high school?"

"No." Suzy's stomach fluttered as she read the stone sign on the front lawn—Edward's High School. And here she was entering tenth grade with a new look, ready to have a great time.

If only classes and homework weren't part of that picture. The flutters turned to rocks. Homework would *not* be fun—a major stressor since she could remember. Even with Dad working with her after dinner many nights, focusing and keeping up the grades had been a struggle.

"Hi, Suzy. Haven't seen you all summer," Sara, a friend from junior high, called as Suzy passed.

"Hey." Suzy smiled but the schoolwork frustrations still played in her mind. She heaved a sigh. Homework battles were a part of life—her life anyway. Maybe other things would make up for it. Like getting in with the popular crowd, amping up the social life.

She and Kaela took the walkway that skirted the office building and led to the center courtyard. There were already long lines. She adjusted her shorts again. Had she stepped out of "plain and ordinary"? When she checked one last time in the mirror before leaving the house, she hoped she had achieved the look—*hot*. But right now her stomach couldn't make up its mind between flutters or rocks.

> **Suzy smiled but the schoolwork frustrations still played in her mind. She heaved a sigh. Homework battles were a part of life.**

Kaela's voice tugged her out of her thoughts. "Do you know any of your classes for sure?"

"No. I hope we get some together."

"Yeah, me too."

They joined one of the lines. While they waited, Suzy scanned the crowd for others she might recognize. She spotted Seth in the next line. OK, so the stomach was leaning toward flutters. She knew Seth from junior high. Blond. Fair skin. Cute nose. Popular. Jock. Cute. Nice. Did she already say *cute*? But he'd never shown much interest in her. Maybe someday—Seth or someone like him. *That's* what this year would be about; she'd make sure of that. The line shifted toward the sign-up tables.

When she checked one last time in the mirror before leaving the house, she hoped she had achieved the look—*hot.*

Seth turned her way and smiled at her. Then his eyebrows rose while he nodded his recognition. "Hi. Wow, you look different."

By his look, that *different* seemed to be good. "Thanks." She smiled back.

She leaned into Kaela. "Seth actually noticed me."

So far, so good—the new Suzy seemed to be working.

A couple of weeks later Suzy, now in the thick of her classes, sat in drama class—first period. She squirmed and her theater-style chair creaked. Her teacher, Mr. Brooks, was picking students to ad-lib a scene. Her seat creaked again, and he looked her way.

Suzy gripped the arms of her chair. *Don't even think of picking me.*

SEDUCED BY SEX : SAVED BY LOVE

A boy raising his hand on the other side of the room caught the teacher's attention instead. "So, you want us to, like, walk up and start a conversation about the other guy's shoes or something?" the boy asked, launching Mr. Brooks into a lecture about spontaneity and allowing everyone to come up with their own ideas. Suzy took a few relieved breaths. *Why did I sign up for this? No homework, but I'll look like an idiot if I get up there.* She scootched down into her seat. *Stay low profile.* She had an idea. She raised her hand.

"You're volunteering, Suzy?"

"No, I need to use the restroom."

"Can't you wait? We're about to ..."

"I really need to go." *I really need to get out of here.*

"Fine. Go."

> **Suzy gripped the arms of her chair.**
> **Don't even think of picking me.**

He seemed frustrated, but what could he say? Suzy pulled up her pack from the floor, pushed out of her chair, and slid past the others in her row to get to the aisle.

When she got outside into the hall, she breathed a sigh of relief and headed toward the restroom. As she passed some classrooms, she looked in open doors to try to spot friends and to break the monotony of the empty hallway.

Which class is Kaela in right now? She thought about their friendship. They'd known each other through junior high. Now they were almost inseparable, hanging out together everywhere—at school, after school, youth club. Yep, everywhere. Well, except church maybe—not Kaela's thing.

Through one doorway she caught the glance of a guy she didn't know. She smiled. He grinned in return and leaned back in his chair to watch her passing. She only wore jeans and a casual green shirt that day. *Something* about her caught his interest. She could get used to this.

She bumped open the restroom door. Forget drama class, homework, and everything else that couldn't keep her attention longer than five minutes. This was gonna be a great year.

Something about her caught his interest. She could get used to this.

"Mom, I'm going out," Suzy called through the house.

Mom poked her head out from the kitchen. "I'll see you at dinner." Suzy noticed her slip off her glasses and wipe her forehead and guessed she had been working hard, as usual. She seemed to always be cleaning or rearranging, always making some corner of the house more beautiful.

Kaela and Suzy stepped out into the gray Washington afternoon. Clouds crept across the sky, teasing of a possible September shower.

Suzy brushed her hair away from her face. "So are we going to Brian's?" She knew the answer. That's what they did since Kaela started hanging out with him.

SEDUCED BY SEX : SAVED BY LOVE

"Yeah." Kaela smiled and nudged her shoulder to Suzy's.

The two girls walked a few steps in silence, then Suzy grabbed her friend and stopped her. "Oh, I forgot to tell you what happened to me today." As they started walking again, she relayed her story about how she escaped drama class and saw the guy who smiled at her. "Do you know who he is?"

"Not sure. You'll have to point him out at school sometime." Kaela nudged Suzy again and the two of them giggled. Then Kaela pulled out a couple of cigarettes. "Want one?"

"Sure." Suzy plucked a cigarette from Kaela's fingers. Her parents didn't approve of smoking, but to her it wasn't that big of a deal. She and Kaela had started in junior high with other friends. Besides, what Suzy did, Kaela did. Or the other way around. She smiled at her friend as she accepted a light.

As they came to Brian's house, they found him leaning on the wall just outside the front door. He dropped his cigarette, rubbed it with his shoe, and pushed himself away from the wall. "We're just watching TV. Come on."

> **Suzy settled into a loveseat nearby. No one really talked. Those who weren't making out stared blankly at the TV.**

His brother and his girlfriend were wrapped in each other's arms on the couch. A few of their friends were sitting on the floor around the smoke-filled room. As Kaela passed Brian, he caught her and kissed her neck, and then together they plopped down at the other end of the couch.

Suzy settled into a love seat nearby. No one really talked. Those who weren't making out stared blankly at the TV. Some reality show was playing on MTV about strangers trying to live together. After a few moments, Kaela and Brian got up from the couch and, still tangled in each other's arms, walked toward the back of the house to Brian's bedroom. Kaela and Brian hadn't been hanging out long, but sex had quickly become a part of their relationship. That was Kaela for you.

In fact, no one seemed to notice much of anything—including her. Fine. She'd just hang out and look tough.

Suzy looked around at the others. No one seemed to notice. In fact, no one seemed to notice much of anything—including her. Fine. She'd just hang out and look tough. Right. She felt anything but.

She slid down into the love seat and pulled her arms across her. She'd have her own boyfriend soon. Kaela did. She would too.

How can a young person live a clean life?
By carefully reading the map of your Word.
I'm single-minded in pursuit of you;
don't let me miss the road signs you've posted.
Psalm 119:10 (The Message)

Impressions. Pressures to fit in. They seemed almost unnoticeable as they slipped one by one into Suzy's mind. She wasn't aware of the false messages behind them; the lure to let go of the things she knew deep down really mattered; how subtly, yet firmly, her values were being shaped and determining her choices.

On the surface, a snapshot of Suzy's life the couple of years before high school didn't look much different from others her age. She enjoyed friends and had a lot of them. She struggled in school but was getting by. Guys were fun to think about and talk about. She got along with her parents most of the time, but generally she was beginning to gravitate more toward her friends for her social life and figuring out her values.

In seventh grade she got involved in a community Christian club for junior highers. At the meetings she had learned about having faith in Jesus and became intrigued by what she read in the Bible. Her mom saw her often choosing to read her Bible over doing her homework: "I felt like she was going to be one of those great spiritual people who can influence others. People listened to her."

But Suzy, like many of her friends, began to live out her faith on the fringes of commitment. Peer pressure led her to compromises that her young faith excused. Others she thought were Christians were doing things. Smoking. Drinking. Playing occult party games. Making out . . . having sex. They seemed to keep their faith separate from how they actually lived. She did too.

As Suzy looked toward entering high school and starting tenth grade, she felt the pressures that go along with entering a new situation. And her goal was to do far more than simply fit in.

She took in the culture around her. She watched her friends. The impressions she picked up told her she had some work to do to measure up.

Maybe some of the friends you're hanging out with aren't cool enough.

You've got to be hot—especially if you want someone like Seth to go for you. You're so plain no one would notice you in front of a white wall.

See the girls in the magazines, in movies, on TV? They've got the style you need, the clothes. They're the ones going to the parties, getting the guys.

You want to look hot? Be popular? You've got some serious work to do if you're going to turn heads when you go to high school this fall.

Something as simple as a TV commercial subtly dictated what it meant to—more than just fit in—be somebody special. Suzy remembered, "It was all about what I looked like and painting the picture the way I thought I'd be accepted." And thinking back on her faith, she said, "I didn't really want to leave *behind* the Christian stuff. I just thought maybe it would work to live in both worlds."

So began a season of living in the moment and responding to what seemed acceptable to those she was hanging out with. And that changed all the time. It would become tough to keep up. It was never her plan that the compromises that seemed so small at first would end up changing the direction of her entire life.

Media and cultural pressures are tough. To those who look up to you, how does your life reflect your responses? When you give someone a compliment, make it one with deeper meaning, one that carries an impact far beyond the messages portrayed in advertising or on the Internet or on TV.

BE COOL

It's subtle, but most of us fall into some sort of a pattern of adapting to our surroundings. We pick up what seems to be acceptable to the people we're around at any given moment. For some, the pressure is over the top. You don't want to stick out or feel uncool. And if you're going to be noticed at all, better make it a good impression. "Popular" would definitely be OK.

But have you noticed—only a few are seen as truly "popular"? And the definition can be debatable.

A group of fourteen- to twenty-two-year-olds expressed what they felt others used to judge popularity potential. At the top of their list was "good looking" or "hot." Next to looks, popularity seemed to come with "being rich," having stuff, or having the right clothes. Have all that and you're in. Others felt it was important to have a boyfriend or girlfriend. Or, some thought, just being seen as "a partier" makes a person popular.

Not shocked, I bet.

Looks a whole lot like some of the messages we hear in our popular culture. What is acceptable or cool is in our faces every day. It influences choices in what we buy, how we use our time, who we'll talk to. It's on the Internet and TV, in movies, magazines, and music. You can't miss it on billboards or in ads in malls. You'll probably see it reflected in the hallways of your school.

And you've probably noticed that popularity or coolness has become a whole lot more than just being about what you look like. It has become what you do. And one of the big messages today is that it's about sex and sensuality.

At sixteen, Stephanie became an alcoholic and started having sex. To her sex was "a way of life," and she believes that "the media has completely normalized sex." She feels that those who want to save sex for marriage can easily feel "ashamed for not going along with the crowd."

Aaron Chidester, a California Bay Area youth pastor who speaks on abstinence, has seen these patterns lots of times. He said, "I really feel that students are living out the reality that's been created by the media, and the media has created such a culture that being sexually active is just the expected thing. It's not that big of a deal anymore that sex takes place more in hook-ups than it does in actual relationships. None of that seems odd anymore." He's also noticed a change in what people view as pornography. Aaron added, "Pornography has basically come out of the back alley. What used to be considered dark, dirty secrets and back-alley stuff is now normal and OK."

Ryan, now twenty, grew up listening to rap music and watching MTV. As early as eight or nine years old he got the impression that "pretty girls danced on tables and slept around." He and his brother would secretly watch a sleazy show on cable

TV. He said, "All the guys were sleeping with girls and then would laugh and joke about it the next day like it was some alpha male contest." The message, Ryan said, was that women are objects and you're not a man unless "you're getting laid."

One of the messages Nicole sees reflected around her every day is, "Have sex *now*. It will satisfy your deepest longings and fix all your problems."

The Internet, music, TV, and other media can have a major influence on what is viewed as normal in sex and relationships. At times, sex is promoted without talking about the consequences. And the consequences can be huge. They just get lost in a living-in-the-moment mentality.

Susan Hicks, a counselor for Christian Encounter Ministries, a residential ministry for at-risk teens, teaches this about living in the moment: "Those who do best in life, no matter what their life situation has been, even to situations [of the worst kinds of abuse], are the ones who can fully tell their story, past and present, while including the future they would like to have." If you bring in a sense of the past and the future into your present choices, you're more likely to think about the consequences.

What happens when you don't? Potentially some pretty hard stuff. Especially if you mix living-in-the-moment thinking with information about "normal" sexuality or "normal" expressions of sensuality that doesn't match up with God's design for intimacy.

Christine picked up that "sex is recreational" and "everybody does it. It's just fun—not a serious thing." She started having sex, both intercourse and oral, by sixteen.

Later, an older boyfriend hired her out as a prostitute and she was also raped.

Kelly said she wanted to look like the women she saw in movies. She said, "When I watched videos, it gave me ideas of how to be sexy and use my body." At fifteen, she was date-raped.

Maybe something like that has happened to you. Maybe it never will. But it's a guarantee that you're impacted on some level by a culture that promotes sensuality. Sex sells. It's been used by marketers to sell nearly everything—even hamburgers. And if you believe anything different from the "norm," as Aaron said, you're likely the one who's considered odd.

Maybe you've felt the culture crunch with some of your views about sex. The message screaming in your face is "Go along with it, or you're not cool."

If only we could collectively crank down the volume on that message and all the others that make sex into something so worthless and cheap.

> **Our culture thrives on what is trendy. When you meet with other youth, talk about how to respond to the pressures that certain trends lay upon us. Encourage one another to be positive trendsetters and, especially, call each other out on behavior that devalues sex or devalues who God created each of us to be.**

Media hype has a way of keeping us trapped in the moment. If many of the messages weren't so far off base, that wouldn't be such a bad thing. But too often they are distorted, especially in their view of who we should be, what we should look like, and how we should think about sex and relationships.

Since media messages are constantly changing, what can keep us grounded? We'll turn again to the group of fourteen- to twenty-two-year-olds, mentioned earlier, who gave their thoughts on what they believed was valued as "popular." They also shared what traits they felt *should be* valued instead. Their top two were *character* and *godliness*. The Bible includes a lot of information about these two qualities, but here are two passages you can take a brief look at now and dig into more later.

Galatians 5:13-25 encourages something called "living by the Spirit" and warns that "the sinful nature desires what is contrary to the Spirit, and the Spirit what is contrary to the sinful nature" (v. 17). Great. Haven't even taken a step, and you've got a battle of natures.

When you read these verses, one section sounds a whole lot like what you might hear and see in the movies, on the Internet, or on TV: sensuality, self-focused living, and the worst of the worst in partying. The other side of things, the "fruit of the Spirit," is made up of nine traits, including kindness, goodness, faithfulness, and self-control (vv. 22-23). The choice: do we let the sinful nature do its thing or do we allow God's Spirit to produce the good stuff in us?

The end of that passage says, "Those who belong to Christ Jesus have crucified the sinful nature with its passions and desires" (v. 24). "Crucified" links the battle to Christ's death on the cross for those sins. When you belong to Christ, the battle against the sinful nature is considered *won*. You may still wrestle, but it's not going to take you under again.

In 2 Peter 1:3-11 we see a reminder that godly living can't be done by our efforts alone. (Whew—that's a good thing.) As we stay connected to God through a relationship with him, his power will help us "participate in the divine nature and escape the corruption of the world caused by evil desires" (2 Peter 1:4). Considering what we face every day, we need that kind of power.

Drop down a little farther in 2 Peter 1 and you'll find a list that shows that good qualities, as part of godly character, build on each other. This is where we do our part: "...make every effort to add to your faith goodness; and to goodness, knowledge; and to knowledge, self-control; and to self-control, perseverance; and to perseverance, godliness; and to godliness, brotherly kindness; and to brotherly kindness, love" (2 Peter 1:5-7). The result of that kind of living? An effective and productive life and a pretty likely bet that you won't fall into the traps of false intimacy (see vv. 8-10).

Whether we're totally aware of it or not, we live by some sort of list of priorities. Where do you get yours? Big picture living keeps in mind that our choices matter every moment. They matter for eternity.

God, sometimes I get so caught up and pressured with what's right in my face that I forget to look past it and remember you are there. Help me shut off the messages of the media or from peers that distort what I should look like or be to others.

Help me turn away from anything that stains the sacredness of your purposes for my life, for sex, and for my relationships. As I instead start to grasp the unchangeable and eternal big picture of what you have in mind for me, guide me in my choices. AMEN.

I am the vine; you are the branches. If a man remains in me and I in him, he will bear much fruit; apart from me you can do nothing.

JOHN 15:5

GOING DEEPER

■ Think about the big *and* the subtle ways sensuality and sex are portrayed in media messages, by your peers, and in your school and church communities. How do those messages compare with what you see as God's design for sex?

■ Look at how you make choices, especially in the areas of relationships and how you view sex. What are the positive influences on your life, and how can you make them more a part of your decisions this week?

■ Big picture living considers how God wants us to live each moment of each day. How can you apply your growing Christian faith to the pressures and messages you hear or see about relationships and sex?

DEEPER STILL

Read Galatians 5 and 2 Peter 1 and create two lists. You might call one the "Spirit-filled nature" and the other the "sinful nature." Make a check mark next to the items in each list that are part of your life. Then, at the bottom of the page, write out the pressures you face and how a Spirit-filled nature will help you stand up to them.

three

I was done with being mediocre and just blending in.
I was so done with it.

"BACHELOR NUMBER ONE? Bachelor number two? Orrrrrr . . . bachelor number three?"

"Pick two! Pick two!" Suzy joined in the chants with the rest of the youth club watching the skit playing out in front of them.

"Two, two, two," Kaela called, and the girls broke into laughter as number two was chosen and then stepped around the divider in nerdy shorts and huge glasses.

The "bachelorette" feigned surprise, then smiled, and hooked her "date's" arm. As the two of them walked off, the other two "bachelors" sagged in over-exaggerated dejection.

The group roared and Suzy smiled as she watched her youth-club friends enjoy the fun. She glanced around the room and then paused to watch her petite friend Camee, head thrown back in laughter, her hands clasped together in front of her. She was a junior this year, a grade older than Suzy. The two of them got to know each other over the last couple of years while they were involved in the junior high youth club. Camee was a true friend. Many of those in the group were just that to Suzy. She felt their acceptance. She fit in.

And yet she wanted more.

She wanted to fit in with her school friends too. That wasn't as easy. But it was why she spent so much time over the summer calculating what it would take. So far it looked like her transformation was working. Now as she walked onto the school campus, she was getting the attention she hoped for. She had more friends. Some makeup, slightly tighter clothes, a little more skin showing—it all helped the cause for popularity. She was beginning to feel the part, but it took work to keep up the image. A lot of work.

Kaela shifted next to her. Her partner in crime: they knew how to enjoy good times without getting caught. Sneaking out at night. Meeting boys. At least she could be anybody she wanted to be around Kaela.

She felt her stomach tighten and glanced up to catch Camee look her way. Could her friend tell what was going on inside right now? The clash she felt—like two different people fighting to be somebody? To be anybody?

The group grew quiet and then settled on the floor and in the chairs and couches of the home where they were meeting. One of the leaders remained standing. *Here comes the serious talk. Someone always does that . . .*

She felt their acceptance. She fit in. And yet she wanted more.

"Before we break up, I want to talk about you and Jesus . . ."

Jesus. She thought back to her first youth-club meeting in the junior high gym. It was October, seventh grade. The students

SEDUCED BY SEX : SAVED BY LOVE

circled around a fake bonfire in the middle of the gymnasium floor and the leader said he had a ghost story to tell. But instead of the usual, scary, campfire story, he talked about Jesus dying and then being resurrected. That night she felt it inside—God wanted her to know him. When the leader talked about the need for forgiveness of sin, she agreed she needed that and accepted Christ as her Savior. It felt so right, so natural—the created coming to her creator. But that was then. Now it felt like the relationship was slipping away.

> **She wanted to be sincere in her longing for God in these meetings and at church, and she often was. But then she would leave him at the door.**

Suzy tuned into the speaker again.

"Do you keep Jesus on a shelf and only take him with you when you need him?" he said. "No, you can't do that. If you've accepted him as your Lord and Savior, he lives here." He tapped his chest. "All the time."

Suzy's own chest ached. She wanted to be sincere in her longing for God in these meetings and at church, and she often was. But then she would leave him at the door.

She bent her head downward and squeezed her eyes to shut off the threatening tears. She was only inviting God where it felt comfortable to have him, when the "Christian" Suzy was around. Otherwise, forget it. He didn't fit in her other world.

Her heart pitched. The truth was smacking her right in the face—stark and convicting. She was one person with Kaela, another with Camee. From one class period to the next, she adjusted who she felt she needed to be depending on who she was talking with. She'd hang out with a tougher crowd, and then she'd do everything she could to avoid being spotted with them. She saw what she was doing. It scared her that she cared less and less.

> The truth was smacking her right in the face—stark and convicting. She was one person with Kaela, another with Camee.

Tears began to burn. Next to her Kaela stretched her legs and squirmed. Likely craving to get out of there, get some food, do anything else but listen to this guy.

Yeah, she was right there with her, but for a different reason. It was getting hard to keep all the different Suzys straight.

A week or so later Suzy was at church. She had wandered down the hall after the youth meeting and saw Camee in one of the classrooms. She just wanted to say hi and Camee had to go and offer to pray for her. What was up with that? Like, did she have *sinner* printed in big letters across her T-shirt?

Camee gathered some papers left from a Bible study, stacked them on the table, then looked toward Suzy. "Are you just going to stand there or are you coming in?"

Suzy kept a firm hold on her position against the doorjamb.

Camee didn't seem fazed by her freeze-out. "So what's going on? You know I care about you."

SEDUCED BY SEX : SAVED BY LOVE

Suzy shrugged. Yes, she knew that, but what could Camee do to help? She was getting in too deep with everything, trying to be a different person in way too many different situations. The compromises were coming faster and easier.

Camee saw through them.

Her friend began to kneel, her small frame a contrast to the fire Suzy saw in her. "I'm going to get down on my knees right here and pray for you whether you like it or not." Camee paused a moment; she seemed to be waiting for a response. "You know, you don't have a choice. God and I are going to fight for you. If you're smart, you'll come and join us."

What was up with that? Like, did she have *sinner* printed in big letters across her T-shirt?

Suzy let out a frustrated puff of breath and rolled her eyes. She pushed away from the door, walked over to where Camee waited, and dropped down to the floor, kneeling beside her. "Go ahead and pray. Maybe it'll do some good." She attempted to appear in control; inside, she was shattering in a million pieces.

As Camee began to pray, she struggled to concentrate. Thoughts invaded. Anxious thoughts. You're-blowing-it thoughts.

Think of something happy. That cute guy, Matt. He was starting to come around her more at school—ever since she and Kaela saw him at the mall and Suzy offered him that cigarette. He seemed to be interested in her. She'd tell Camee about him after the prayer . . . Or maybe not. Camee'd only warn her not to start anything with this guy. She'd probably be right. Suzy sighed and pressed her arms into her stomach.

As Camee began to pray, she struggled to concentrate. Thoughts invaded. Anxious thoughts. You're-blowing-it thoughts.

Camee continued to pray as more thoughts flitted through Suzy's mind. Something in Camee's prayer triggered another memory—that day she was practicing to run the 800 and a Bible verse kept repeating in her mind: "He who watches over Israel will neither slumber nor sleep" (Psalm 121:4). It had made an impression because she didn't realize she knew the verse. Was God trying to remind her he was with her, watching over her? *God, are you still watching over me?*

Tears threatened. *Control the emotions.* Suzy pulled in a slow breath and rubbed her arms. Through her sleeves she felt the sting of recent burns and cuts. Last year, she had started to purposely hurt herself—but only once in awhile. Lately, she turned to it more often. It seemed to give her the control she craved. Sometimes it offered punishment—something she believed she deserved right now. Her life was a screwed-up mess. Anxiety shook her from deep inside. So much for control.

She felt Camee's hand on her shoulder and lifted her head.

"You can talk to me anytime, 'kay?" Camee's voice was calm, but her eyes screamed concern.

SEDUCED BY SEX : SAVED BY LOVE

Suzy pushed back the tears and nodded. "Thanks." She rubbed her arm again. The prayer helped, but she felt a clash of emotions. She wanted out of there.

At home Suzy went straight to her room and closed her door. The anxiety lashed its way to the surface; self-condemnation fired shots at her. Who was she trying to be anyway? At church she felt the yearning inside to feel God's closeness again, but what did he think of her? Her different faces couldn't fool him. He knew the real Suzy.

> ## She'd tell Camee about him after the prayer . . . Or maybe not.

She popped in a CD. As disharmonic tones and dark words about anger and loneliness filled her room, she opened her window and lit a cigarette. She'd need to make it through or surrender to the craving to cut herself. She thought of the serrated knife hidden in her armoire. The music pounded until she could no longer distinguish what was shaking—the bass vibrations from the music . . . or her. She took another drag on her cigarette.

Stop. Stop feeling.

> Then Jesus said, "Come to me, all of you who are weary and carry heavy burdens, and I will give you rest."
> MATTHEW 11:28 (NLT)

Suzy's confidence had wavered. It was beginning to crumble entirely. One moment she felt at the top of her game, the next like her efforts could never be enough. She desperately wanted to settle into a skin she could feel comfortable with. It wasn't happening.

At school she especially felt the pressure: "I had started the nice-girl-Christian-thing around my (youth-club) friends, and then having another face to any other popular people around." Not surprisingly, Suzy began to feel like she was losing herself. She said, "That's the danger of trying to be a people pleaser. I was trying so hard to be somebody else during every class—and there were seven class periods. You know, it gets exhausting and you don't think about the consequences at all, because everything is in the moment."

Camee remembers noticing the change in Suzy: "She started dressing more provocatively. She wore tighter clothes and a lot of makeup. She presented herself very differently. She wanted to be seen by guys. As a teenager myself, I didn't see that they were signs of anything that was bad or wrong. I just thought, 'Something's different about Suzy.'"

In Camee's eyes, Suzy was well-liked at their youth club and at church. She said, "She was very, very loved, very accepted." But at the same time, she saw Suzy's choice of friends changing. "I remember there were a couple guys that I could see she was getting closer with—they were on the line. They would say they were Christians and they were in the Christian crowd, but they were kind of the rebel guys. I could see that Suzy was gravitating toward hanging out with them more when we were in our (youth-club) crowd. But I didn't really see her much at our high school."

Suzy made sure of that.

Of her faith at that time Suzy said, "My Christianity was very superficial. I don't know that I had a personal walk. It was more social."

In her struggles and self-confessed rebellion, she refused to turn to her parents. Even if she was willing to include them, she didn't know how to express all that was going on inside. She said, "Maybe I could have been honest with my parents, but for some reason I didn't take that route. I was afraid to let the real me be known to anyone, and I lost myself in that."

Suzy continued to struggle with schoolwork too. That pressure, with the demands she felt from herself and others to fit in, led to intense anxiety. Self-injury that had only been an occasional thing became an option she turned to more and more. She said, "I felt I had to have some sense of control of my totally chaotic social life, and cutting was how I took control." Her need for acceptance catapulted her into a time of losing track of who she really was. She found herself falling headlong into more self-destructive choices.

Searching for a sense of security in false intimacy was just around the corner.

Give the teens and young adults in your life the opportunities to talk about the chaos and pressures in their lives. Figure out healthy ways to handle anxiety. For example, talking to someone, playing sports, or doing creative activities. Encourage such expressions. Get to know your friend better by joining them in these activities.

WHO AM I? WHERE DO I BELONG?

Suzy's image at any given moment was defined by what she thought was valued by the different people she hung out with. It was becoming more and more defined by those she saw as being in the popular crowd. She changed her makeup, the way she dressed, and who she hung out with. The problem was that it never felt quite right. Who was she? Where did she belong? What would she have to do next to fit in? She was moving into dangerous waters—doing whatever it would take.

We want to belong. And depending on our personalities, we work hard to either blend in or stand out—whatever makes us feel we fit. Sometimes solid values are sacrificed. Sometimes what gets sacrificed is *me*.

Ryan had been at a party with friends, and it seemed like the atmosphere and conversation constantly focused on sex. His friends kept talking to him about "getting laid." Just to keep their approval, that night he slept with a girl he didn't really know. Looking back, he doesn't feel he fully realized what he got caught up in, but he said, "I did know I basically just wanted to say I did it."

Alyssa had what she considered a pretty normal childhood. She enjoyed school and friends, but in some ways she felt it was too easy. She said, "My values weren't that challenged. I never had to think too much about what they were."

Going into junior high her parents divorced and she moved to another state with her mom and began attending a junior high known for its rough reputation. She found friends and did well in school, but she also began to feel a growing pressure to fit in. Friends who seemed to share her values were changing. She said, "By my second year there my friends began to compromise with smoking, alcohol, drugs, making out with guys. To an extent, I followed—partly by choice and not having a solid feel for what I valued, and partly because one of my 'best' friends threatened to beat me up if I tried to find new friends. Or she threatened to beat up the new friend."

Alyssa's grades began to suffer. She got kicked off the cheerleading squad. She was emotionally drained. "Really, I was just barely surviving. I felt caught up in something I didn't fully like and definitely didn't know how to get out of." She thought she'd get a fresh start when she was assigned to a different high school from her friends, but the hurt and confusion had gone deep. "Once outgoing, now I was quiet. I struggled to figure out who I was. I tripped through trying on different images with different groups of friends."

Some of those friends told her about Jesus. She said, "I didn't know Jesus cared about who I was. I discovered that he wanted to remove the mess I had created in my life, and I asked for his forgiveness. He became my Savior and my Lord."

She now sees that as a defining moment. "I didn't notice it at the time, but later, when I looked back, I saw very clearly how that was the moment when I began to know who I really was and where I really belonged."

> Borrow a boat anchor to use as a visual and talk with teens and young adults about their values on media, sex, and relationships. Discuss how to develop strong, solid anchors for those values— ones that stand up to cultural pressures.

Only One Real Me

Even in a culture that may pressure you to be pretty, be cool, be sexy, be loose, to be lots of things to feel worthwhile, there's another message going around out there: Be authentic. Be real.

It's a good challenge. Realness helps us think about what we're doing and saying and how that matches up with who we are. It can even help us feel more comfortable about going against the grain of current trends when those don't fit God's standard for our lives. But your realness or authenticity should go deep or it won't stand up for long or have much meaning. It needs an anchor in something real and lasting.

Here's an anchor: You were created by God, in the image of God (Genesis 1:26, 27) and, in being formed in that image, you have a purpose (Colossians 1:16-18).

At the core of who we are is the image of God. We forget that. In all the pressure of the stuff that is thrown at us each day, we see other images that we feel a need to try to become. In choices we make, including sexual activity apart from God's original design, we lose sight of who God intended us to be. As with Suzy, it never feels quite right. It can't, because we were created to live and breathe the image of God, to reflect his character in every way we can. When we don't, and we're paying attention, we feel it. Something's wrong.

We can get back to what's intended for our lives by spending time getting to know God and the image we were created in. Specifically, reading the Bible and keeping in mind the question, "What does this tell me about God's character?" helps us do that. Another way is by getting to know Jesus deeply— how he walked on earth and faced temptations, how he loved people in real ways that honored who they were, how he faced major struggles, even death, as he stayed true to his purpose and who he was. He sacrificed a lot, but didn't give up one ounce of who he was created to be.

You don't have to sacrifice any part of who you were created to be, either. God knows you and sees all of who you are. Not the ugly, fake stuff others push on you that you might have tried on, but the real you and the potential you that is amazing.

God, it's so easy to take on some expected image without even knowing I did, and then to start compromising the image you have in mind for me. Help me see clearly the ways I've been willing to believe lies or to compromise in ways that messes that up, and show me how to take steps back to you. I want to know your Son, Jesus, and through him to know who I am and where I belong. AMEN.

> So then, just as you received Christ Jesus as Lord, continue to live in him, rooted and built up in him, strengthened in the faith as you were taught, and overflowing with thankfulness. See to it that no one takes you captive through hollow and deceptive philosophy, which depends on human tradition and the basic principles of this world rather than on Christ.
>
> COLOSSIANS 2:6-8

GOING DEEPER

■ In thinking about God creating you in his image, for his purposes, how would you answer these questions: Who am I? Where do I belong?

■ Think about the situations in which you find it hard to be yourself. What are some of your qualities—that come from being made in God's image—that are worth developing and not hiding?

■ What are the ways that knowing you are created in the image of God will help you not compromise sexually?

DEEPER STILL

Your mirror reflects what's on the outside. What counts more is what's on the inside. Write down different qualities you have that you know are a reflection of God living inside of you. You can write these directly on your mirror or write them on index cards and keep them where you'll see them often. Remind yourself of those qualities before you walk out the door each morning. Plan to live them out.

four

It's hard to explain, but I had a lot of 'I've been raped' feelings, so it was really easy to convince people of the lie and go along with it myself.

"IT'S NOTHING." Suzy knelt near Troy's locker and shoved her dropped books into her backpack. As she did, she pushed the serrated knife farther out of sight. It hadn't fallen out with the books, but had Troy spotted it and figured out what was going on?

She and Troy had gone out a couple of times, were just good friends. When she got to school that morning, she had reached into her pack to loan him a pen and some of her books spilled. When she bent down, her sleeves came up. He asked her about the burns on her arms and the gash on her leg. She didn't want to talk about it.

She stood and pulled the backpack over her shoulder. She noticed he was still staring at her, probably waiting for an explanation. "What?"

"So how'd you get hurt?" His eyes darted to her backpack.

She shifted the weight of her pack behind her. "I told you, it's nothing."

"OK. I gotta get to class. I'll talk to you later." He gave an upward nod and turned.

She watched him walk away. He didn't act like he believed her, but at least he let it go.

Suzy went to her Spanish class and then to science, dragging herself through the day. She only had one class left to get through—algebra. She slumped into her desk, waiting for it to start so it could be over and she could go home.

> **"So how'd you get hurt?"**
> **His eyes darted to her backpack.**
> **She shifted the weight of her pack behind her.**
> **"I told you, it's nothing."**

Her teacher talked on and on about negative exponents, or something. Whatever it was, she didn't understand . . . or care. She realized how tired of everything she felt—the pressures every day, keeping up with school, but even more in keeping up with what it took to fit in. Her changed image worked with some people, but it was still an image. Pouring everything into it drained her.

Someone next to her poked her. "Suzy, they meant you."

"What do you mean?"

"The loudspeaker. They called you to the main office."

Now the adrenaline was flowing. She was alert. *Why do they want—? Troy. He turned me in.* She shoved her math book into her pack, slammed through the door, and headed to the office.

She slowed. What were they going to ask? She thought of the fresh injuries on her legs and arms. How would she get out of there without explaining the cuts and burns? She couldn't very well tell them she'd taken the knife and ripped the flesh of her leg, or that she'd pushed the lit end of cigarettes into her arms. Like they'd understand that. They'd want to know why and that was something she couldn't explain. That and the knife that was still in her backpack.

She just wouldn't tell them anything. She stepped up to the receptionist's desk.

"Mrs. Brewer is waiting for you in the counseling room." The woman pointed toward a short hallway.

Suzy walked down the hall and stepped into an office on the left. She was surprised to see her parents. She checked their expressions. She expected *mad* since she had been arguing and talking back more lately, but they looked more sad and worried. "Go ahead and have a seat, Suzy," the counselor said, as she pointed to the one empty chair.

Suzy hesitated for just a moment, then sat, dropping her pack to the floor.

> **Now the adrenaline was flowing.**
> **She was alert. *Why do they want—?***

The school counselor, Mrs. Brewer, with her dark shoulder-length hair just beginning to gray, seemed about her mom's age. She tugged the bottom edge of her suit jacket and watched Suzy for a moment before she spoke again.

"I understand that you have injuries on your arms and your leg, and some friends have been concerned about how you got those," the counselor said. "You brought a knife to school."

Troy.

Mrs. Brewer's voice softened. "I called your parents. Could you tell us what's going on?"

four

Suzy crossed her arms and stared at the floor.

The counselor continued. "How'd you get hurt? Did someone hurt you?"

What can I tell them? They'll never understand me hurting myself.

"Did you bring the knife to protect yourself?"

She saw where Mrs. Brewer was going with this. Maybe if she went along, they'd leave her alone. Her whole body tensed. She didn't like to lie.

> **Silence again. She was getting really familiar with the marbled white and black patterns of the linoleum floor.**

Her dad sat forward. "Did someone hurt you?"

Oh no, where do I go with that? Silence again. She was getting really familiar with the marbled white and black patterns of the linoleum floor.

The counselor prodded gently. "Tell us what happened."

Then the words poured out before she could think through what she was saying. "I snuck out one night and was over here by the high school. Some guy drove up in his car and stopped me. He had a knife. He held it to me and raped me, and then he cut me."

There it was in one breath. And it *felt* so true.

Dad rubbed his hand through his thick, graying hair. "I wondered if something like this had happened."

"Oh, honey." Mom reached toward her.

SEDUCED BY SEX : SAVED BY LOVE

Mrs. Brewer wanted more. "Did you recognize the guy? What kind of car was it?" She paused, but not long. "Did he just leave you there? How'd you get away?"

"I don't know. I don't remember. I . . ." The diversion was totally backfiring—*now what?* Suzy kept her head down. "Can I just go home now?"

"Yes, I think we should." Mom seemed to want this over as much as she did.

But Mrs. Brewer wasn't finished. "We'll need to report this. And you'll need to take her to the hospital for an examination."

Suzy froze. The report part was bad enough but . . . "I don't want an examination."

"That's understandable. It's normal not to want to be examined after a . . . a rape. It's for your safety, however." The counselor was trying to reassure her, but Suzy felt anything but assured.

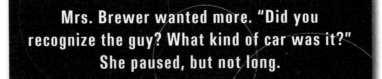

Mrs. Brewer wanted more. "Did you recognize the guy? What kind of car was it?" She paused, but not long.

"We'll wait until morning." Her mom seemed to be saying that as much to Mrs. Brewer as she was to her daughter.

Suzy sighed. She'd have to go along with the examination and hope the lie would quickly play itself out. At least they didn't figure out she was the one who inflicted the burns and gashes. One on her calf still bled.

The next morning was a nightmare, just trying to get through the humiliating examination—and knowing it was meant to find evidence for something that never happened.

"OK, we're done. Go ahead and get dressed and come out when you're ready." The nurse left the room.

Suzy sat up, scooted off the exam table, and began to untie the awkward gown they'd given her. She hoped her charade would be over after this, but she could tell it wasn't going to be. It was just one more thing to go with all the other pretending she had been doing. She didn't like any of it. She felt she had fallen into some dark hole and was plunging deeper and deeper with each waking hour. She pulled on her jeans.

Rape. The examination would show no signs of it, but there was something about it that rang true. For a long time she had been feeling raped anyway—that menacing sense of violation. She shivered as images of a closet and an older neighbor boy flashed through her mind. It was so long ago. She was only four. And other vague memories troubled her. There was more she couldn't remember. She didn't want to.

> *Rape.* The examination would show no signs of it, but there was something about it that rang true.

Her jeans scraped her injured leg and she winced. She felt she deserved that pain—and more. Especially now. She had lied.

Over the next few weeks, Suzy walked the thin edge of performance—at home, at church, at school. Pressures continued. The lie lived on. She cut and burned herself. Fought for acceptance. Performed. Cut more.

Matt brought her into his circle, and she believed she might be finally finding her way toward the acceptance she was going for. But one more thing to do. It was expected. Everyone does it. Don't think. Just do it.

Matt.

A garage.

A bed.

Her life changed. Forever.

> **You let the world, which doesn't know the first thing about living, tell you how to live. You filled your lungs with polluted unbelief, and then exhaled disobedience.**
>
> EPHESIANS 2:2 (THE MESSAGE)

BEHIND THE SADNESS

Suzy's self-injury and her lie were signs of her inner world—the painful struggle to gain control, to fit in, to make sense of things that went far deeper than she could grasp.

"The cutting was my way of controlling some emotions, my way of crying out for help without words. So the cutting—I knew people saw it, and I was also lashing out at myself for not knowing how to pull it together." It had other uses for her too. For one, it was a way for her to manage the emotions of not meeting expectations—from her peers, from herself, from her family.

Home had its challenges. Her father was in the military, and the family traveled to Germany and Turkey before it settled back in the US when she was six. She had two older brothers, one fifteen years older and the other ten years older. Her brothers added their own struggling dynamics into the mix before and after they were out on their own. Looking back at her home life, Suzy said, "We didn't know how to communicate. We swept things under the carpet—made everything look beautiful. We even had a room called the Pretty Room." This was their living room, used mostly for guests, sometimes to relax and watch TV.

Suzy took her place in keeping up the family image. "When something is wrong in your family, you can't advertise it. You don't do that. And I didn't meet my parents' approval in some areas, and so . . . so I cut on myself."

The reasons went even deeper. As Suzy told the lie about the rape, part of her screamed that she really had been violated and it was *not* over. Swept far back into her memory were instances of childhood molestations by non-family members, boys who were older than her. Other instances of possible molestation, that others have told her about but she can't recall, are still confusing for her to this day.

From those experiences and what she watched in her peers and the culture around her, sex didn't mean much to anyone. It was just an act, a tool. For her, it became a way of gaining attention and belonging. But it was also a part of her self-injury. "Having sex was another way to cut on myself," she said. She lived with the blurred and distorted reminders that she didn't deserve to be treated any better.

> Be aware if someone you're around talks about abuse or seems to act as if they are being abused—by family members, peers, someone they're dating, anyone. Don't ignore those possible signs. Your friend could be in an emergency situation and need intervention. Help them connect to strong resources, including pastors or counselors. If needed, report the matter to authorities.

THE PAST IN THE PRESENT

Like Suzy, your mind-set about yourself, your choices, or your values might have been partially shaped by your past, whether or not you are fully aware of it. If you're making self-destructive choices, including stepping into sexual relationships before marriage, you may have deep wounds and misconceptions about yourself that are driving you to that place.

Justin's parents divorced and he lived part-time with each parent. His father was a drug addict. As far back as Justin can remember, pornography was all over the walls of his dad's house, on the TV, and available in magazines. Even as a child, he knew it was wrong. Of those images, he said, "I'm seeing this woman and she doesn't have any clothes on, and I'm not supposed to see that. It taught me that women are objects." The first time he had sex was in the back of a truck with a girl he'd known for two weeks.

Kelly's dad was an alcoholic who abused her mom. In her eyes, Dad only wanted her mom for sex and often grabbed her inappropriately in front of Kelly. She grew up longing to know her worth. At fifteen she was date-raped. After that, sex became a part of her partying lifestyle, leading to another rape.

Reese was placed in a foster care home at the age of ten. He went from innocent boyhood into a world of prejudice, violence, drugs, sex, and alcohol. Not long after he arrived in his new "home," he was beaten and raped by guys in the neighborhood. The message he learned quickly was that "it wasn't a big deal to give yourself away sexually, to be into drugs and alcohol—just a way to fit in." At the age of twelve he got drunk and had sex with a girl whose name he no longer remembers. By fourteen he had had sex with three more girls.

Christine's father abused her verbally and mentally. She said, "My father looked at me and spoke to me like I was a sex object, even when I was very young. He also engrained in me that I had no right to stand up for myself. I was expected to keep quiet and allow myself to be treated like dirt." She was later sexually abused and raped.

These situations may sound extreme to you. Maybe not. But we all have experiences and impressions that have shaped us—including our view of our worth, and our perspectives on sex and relationships. Counselor Susan Hicks puts it this way: "God had his design and it worked. When those designs, or 'maps,' get broken or damaged, kids inherit that damage, and so they carry around a different map."

Look closely at how your past is impacting your life right now. Don't consider any of it too small to address. You're too important to God for that. And what he has in mind for you to one day enjoy is an intimacy that is far better than you can imagine. Don't let anything rob you of that. Including your past.

> As someone involved in your friend or family member's life, you are a part of creating their "past." Think about the importance of that; be responsible and careful with your words and actions.

ON TO SOMETHING NEW

Our past moves in and takes up residence in our hearts—for good or bad—and so it is a big part of developing the heart we bring to God. He can create something new there, something hopeful.

Galatians 5:1 says, "It is for freedom that Christ has set us free. Stand firm, then, and do not let yourselves be burdened again by a yoke of slavery." A part of the yoke for the Galatians was rules and legalism, but our yoke can be anything in our past that hangs around our neck and keeps us trapped in a life we don't want. Abuse, lack of love and acceptance, confusing values, even our own choices—weeks, months, years ago—affect the way we live our life today. But those things can change.

"It is for freedom that Christ has set us free." We don't have to let the past enslave us. It can be redeemed and used by God for the present and for our future. The part we don't have to take into the future is the negative or false messages we've received from others, or our pattern of destructive choices.

A passage in Ephesians says, "You were taught, with regard to your former way of life, to put off your old self, which is being corrupted by its deceitful desires; to be made new in the attitude of your minds; and to put on the new self, created to be like God in true righteousness and holiness" (Ephesians 4:22-24). We can take off our old patterns of living just like a person would take off old, dirty, torn-up clothes. We can put on the new self—created to be like God, righteous and holy.

Why keep wearing the old when you've got something new? God wants that newness, that restoration, to get deep into your heart. That's the place of hope. The place of freedom.

God, only you know my greatest struggles, my deepest pain. And only you can heal those. I don't want my past to keep a hold on me in a way that leads to choices that only cause more hurt. Forgive me. Heal me. Free me. AMEN.

Therefore, if anyone is in Christ, he is a new creation; the old has gone, the new has come!
2 CORINTHIANS 5:17

■ Your past might include distorted family dynamics, abuse, self-esteem struggles that led you into the arms of false intimacy, using pornography, or peer influences that have harmed or confused you. How have these things twisted your view of God's design for relationships and sex?

■ Think of how experiences from your past might still be clinging and showing up in your attitudes about yourself, or in how you might gravitate toward risky situations. What can you do differently right now to take hold of the freedom you have in Christ?

■ The past can be engrained so strongly that we have trouble responding in a good way to pressure from others. In the area of relationships, and possibly in temptations to sex, what situations are most difficult for you? What's one key action you can take to be better prepared to respond to those situations next time?

DEEPER STILL

Now that you've taken a look at your past and how it affects you today, make a quick list of those things that are painful, or at least difficult to deal with, that you feel about yourself. To help "take off" that past in your life in a tangible way, rip up the list and throw it away.

Now write a prayer to God, as you "put on" this new attitude: I am created to be like God in true righteousness and holiness.

five

*Had I known I was valuable without doing those things,
I wouldn't have done them.*

"A BUNCH OF US ARE HANGING OUT over at Nate's. You and Kaela want to come?"

Hearing Matt's voice made Suzy's heart skip a beat. Their relationship was over after someone saw her at a party making out with one of Matt's friends, and then word got back to Matt. Totally stupid. It didn't mean anything, but it ended things with Matt. But then they didn't have much going for them in their relationship anyway. At least he wasn't mad anymore or he wouldn't be calling.

"Just a sec. Let me ask Kaela." Suzy put her hand over her phone and checked to see what her friend wanted to do. Kaela was usually up for anything. Suzy told her what the guys were asking. Kaela, lying on Suzy's bedroom floor and flipping through an issue of *Teen* magazine, didn't hesitate.

Suzy uncovered the phone. "Sure."

"OK, Josh and I will pick you guys up."

As the four of them walked into Nate's house, Suzy noticed some of Matt's other friends sitting around the den. Open bottles of alcohol and half-empty glasses sat on the counter and coffee table. No other girls? Guess it didn't matter. They were just hanging out. Nate's mom passed through. They might as well have been invisible. She didn't seem to care what they were doing.

"How's it going?" Josh grinned somewhat shyly at Suzy. "You want some Jose Cuervo?"

"What?"

"Tequila."

She'd try anything once ... or twice. "Sure." She sat down on the couch near Josh as he handed her the bottle. No glass? She shrugged. Suzy tipped her head back and took in a mouthful of the clear liquid. It burned going down, but also tasted sweet and strong.

> No other girls? Guess it didn't matter.
> They were just hanging out.
> Nate's mom passed through.
> They might as well have been invisible.

She heard laughter and turned to see Kaela falling into the lap of one of the guys. As she watched the scene, she felt her head growing lighter. She laughed too. When she turned back, Josh was sitting closer, leaning toward her. She could smell the alcohol on his breath. She sipped more of the tequila and watched the scene around her. Everyone was getting drunk. A distant caution pricked at her thoughts, but it blurred quickly and was gone.

Josh put his arms around her and kissed her neck. It was now easy to give in and respond. She slid into his lap. As she did, she heard Matt's slurred voice in her ear: "You'll be Josh's first."

SEDUCED BY SEX : SAVED BY LOVE

She looked up and Matt was gone, but she saw Kaela and her guy laughing and tripping down the hallway toward the bedrooms.

> **She heard laughter and turned to see Kaela falling into the lap of one of the guys. As she watched the scene, she felt her head growing lighter.**

Then Josh was standing and pulling her up with him. The room spun as he drew her toward the hallway. She followed.

The next moments swirled by in a mixture of tequila dizziness and sex. His first but not hers—that was gone. Even in her lightheaded state, she felt sadness welling deep inside. She had lied about her self-inflicted injuries, and some believed she had been raped. The lie had taken on life and spread. So now she was marked. *Why not make it all true? Punish myself for telling it . . . like going to Matt's that day.* The thought startled her: *Am I punishing myself? Could that be part of the reason I had sex with Matt?* Her heart wrenched and she groaned.

She sat up, and her stomach pitched. Josh was leaving the room. Where was he going? As she began pulling on her jeans, she noticed through her stupor that Matt was now in front of her.

"I'm next." There appeared to be a lazy smile on his face as he pushed her back onto the bed. Her soul cried and then fell silent as Matt took his turn with her. At moments she felt the battle inside. *You deserve better. . . . No you don't—this is what you chose.*

five

The time passed in hazy emotional agony. She tried to shut down the internal accusations, and found herself detaching to survive. *It doesn't matter. It's only sex. It doesn't mean anything. I don't mean anything.*

> **Even in her lightheaded state,
> she felt sadness welling deep inside.
> She had lied about her self-inflicted injuries,
> and some believed she had been raped.
> The lie had taken on life and spread.**

She heard muffled voices on the other side of the closed door—arguing.

Matt rolled off the bed and started to dress.

She pulled on her clothes and opened the door.

Kaela was there, grabbing Suzy's arm. "Let's go."

She was still plenty buzzed. "Why? What's—?"

"We're going right *now*." Kaela was mad. "Matt, take us home."

When the two got back to Suzy's house, she wanted to know what had gotten Kaela so hot.

"What ticked me off? You should have—" She heaved a sigh. "Oh, forget it. If you don't . . ."

"Tell me. What happened? Did someone hurt you?"

"Nothing happened to *me*. Don't you know what was going on there?" Kaela was steaming. "If you had stayed, every one of those guys would have ended up in that room with you."

SEDUCED BY SEX : SAVED BY LOVE

Suzy drew in a quick breath and sat down on her bed. Kaela stood there with arms crossed. Suzy began to grasp what was going on behind that glare. "You stopped them, didn't you?"

"*Yes*, I stopped them."

Suzy steadied herself, her mind beginning to free itself of the tequila. Closing her eyes, she let her head drop back. She saw it now. Josh, then Matt, then—what would have been next? *Who* would have been next? She shook her head, swallowed. She deserved it. She'd made that first choice with Matt only weeks ago. Then every date or party since involved someone with those kinds of expectations—not sex, but not far from it either. That's how they saw her now—easy. This isn't at all what she wanted when she started going after that new image.

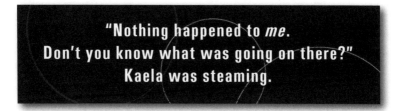

"Nothing happened to *me*.
Don't you know what was going on there?"
Kaela was steaming.

She felt nauseated and it had nothing to do with the alcohol. She looked at Kaela still standing there, seething. Suzy looked away and flinched at the pain in her heart.

She'd have to shut that down before she crumbled.

> Free me from the trap that is set for me,
> for you are my refuge.
> Psalm 31:4

A shell. An object. A toy.

That's how Suzy now saw her body. So that's how she thought guys saw her. She used her body to get attention, to be accepted. They used her body for sex.

No one thought of the person who was dying inside.

She really did begin to feel like just an object to be used by others. "I was only skin deep. Sex meant nothing to me anymore," Suzy remembered later. And changing her course didn't cross her mind. "I was so given into that lifestyle at that point—I don't know—I wasn't looking at the consequences. I wasn't able to. And that's a really dangerous place. It snowballed for me really easily."

She remembers that season of her life with deep sadness and still some shame. "I walked into a lifestyle where the more I did it, the less I cared about myself, and the more I wanted to beat myself up and give more of myself away."

"I gave myself away"—those words get used a lot. For Suzy, they have deep meaning. "God has forgiven me, but . . . sometimes I think back to the situations I put myself in. And because I have those memories, because they are a part of me, it forever changed my life, forever affected me. When I'm ninety I will still have those memories. People don't realize that; they don't realize how permanent those kinds of decisions are. You can't get that innocence back."

She knows. The forgiveness Suzy has experienced is very real—but so are the memories.

God's design for sex needs to be openly discussed. There needs to be more to the message than "sex before marriage is wrong." Read about it. Study it in the Bible. Communicate its importance. Live it out with conviction.

Honoring

Being molested twice when she was a little girl led Suzy to view herself in distorted ways. She had come to see sex only as something you do, or something that is done to you. It didn't have much meaning beyond that. But that view is so far from God's intention for sex—an expression of love within marriage, a bonding with one person, a part of enjoying getting to know one person intimately in every way. Suzy had no idea that sex was a gift for two people to enjoy, an intimacy without shame.

When sex is used in other ways, it's going to feel empty and unsatisfying. It would be some time before Suzy would fully grasp that her body and emotions were crying out for her to stop. Her hope is that others won't walk the same path she did, but if they do, that they can find a way back. "There are girls out there who have been used and have let themselves be treated that way, and now they feel like trash. They need to know there's hope, healing, forgiveness—life after the state they've been in. Newness."

Many do find that newness. Nicole, who was sexually abused from age three and then became sexually active at seventeen, is finding healing through learning her worth in God's sight. She said, "I'm learning how to share my heart and my mind more and seeing that that is valuable." And she is finding, in a current relationship, that her boundaries can be respected and that she is still loved.

Grasp the gift and value of sex as God intended it. Grab hold of the truth of your personal value. You're worth much more than just being used as an object. You're worth the beautiful, mysterious, and sacred gift of a union that God has for you and your future spouse.

And it's not just about us. When we keep in mind God's intention and timing for sex, we know that others are worth honoring, not violating in any way. Sex before marriage *always* dishonors the other person. Dressing to attract and to stir up emotions and hormones, touching, talking, inviting sexual thoughts or activities—all dishonor.

Stephanie learned at a young age that her femininity had power. "It became an art for me to hook guys and use them to meet my needs," she said. "I didn't think of them and how my behavior affected their spirit and soul."

Another way to think of it is to consider that the other person is someone's future spouse. Check yourself. Consider your words, actions, behavior, and thoughts toward the opposite sex. Every bit of it matters. If you're crossing lines and not honoring that person, it's a problem.

It's a lot about watching ourselves to see if we're being selfish and using someone else for our own pleasure. We could call it "exploiting," because essentially that's what it is.

Ryan, who was raised with the belief that he needed to get out there and have sex, has learned to see women very differently. "When I look at a girl, instead of looking at her with lust, I remember she is a child of God, just as I am. She is worth something and special to God. I don't see her as an object of just 'easy fun.'"

When you begin to see yourself and others differently, the way God views us, it will impact the situations you choose to be in, how you honor yourself, and how you honor someone else. It's a great discovery.

Capture an honoring mentality and be an example to others. How do you treat the opposite sex? How do you dress? How do you talk to them or about them? Do you honor them as Christ would?

'LOVE AND HONOR' NOW

"Treat others with respect." It's a common phrase. But the thing is, we don't always do that. There's something about sex. When the thought of it gets in our minds and stirs up the hormones, we can get pretty selfish. We let that desire control us instead of controlling *it*, and it quickly turns into all-about-me time.

It's no surprise that the Bible teaches something totally different and something totally better. Romans 12:10 says, "Be devoted to one another in brotherly love. Honor one another above yourselves." Devotion? That's a committed action. Two people are involved, with respect and honor flowing both ways.

five

No room for disrespect or abuse in either direction, only caring about the other person on a respectful, honoring level. Think of it as if that other person is your physical sister or brother.

Jesus put it this way: "So now I am giving you a new commandment: Love each other. Just as I have loved you, you should love each other" (John 13:34, *NLT*).

Loving others as Jesus would. That's a huge standard, but that's what we're called to do. When you think of that within the context of God's design and timing for sex, it only makes sense. Besides, wouldn't your future spouse love it if, while you're saving sex for marriage, you practiced honoring others as Jesus would? No question.

> *God, I admit it's hard for me to naturally honor*
> *someone or love them as Jesus would. It's especially*
> *hard when I get off track with my emotions or desires.*
> *Help me stay focused on you. Help me learn how*
> *to value others the way you do and to value myself*
> *as well. Help me grow in self-control and caring*
> *for others in ways that build them up.* AMEN.

You, my brothers, were called to be free. But do not use your freedom to indulge the sinful nature; rather, serve one another in love.

GALATIANS 5:13

GOING DEEPER

■ Are there ways you've been treated as less than a person of value by significant people in your life? How does that affect the way you allow yourself to be treated in relationships with the opposite sex?

■ Reflect on your ideas about sexual intimacy. When you consider how God wants us to honor ourselves and others, in what ways can you change your thinking so that it impacts your choices from now on?

■ Emotions and desires are real and natural, but at the same time some of them can lead down dangerous paths if we choose to follow them. What are ways you can keep emotions in check and honor others?

five

DEEPER STILL

One way you can honor yourself and others *and* keep your emotions and desires in check is to focus on activities that develop your God-given strengths and that serve others. Over the next few days, make a list of these kinds of activities. Choose one thing from your list and go after it.

six

I just couldn't keep up with myself anymore. Reaching out was the only thing I had—the hope that someone else would respond to my desperation and my need for help was all I had left.

SUZY HUDDLED INTO THE WALL. Sitting on her floor near her closet, she curled her legs in close to her trembling body. She couldn't escape the intensity she felt to cut herself again. A broken light bulb was in reach under a nearby wastebasket. She had scratched her forearm with its jagged edge and then put it out of her reach, afraid of what she'd do next.

Sadness pressed in. Anger and fear shook her. All she could think of was the mess she'd made of her life—a life she felt she'd thrown away through messed-up choices. *Life—why not just . . . ?*— No. She didn't want to go there with her thoughts. Tears turned to sobs.

She grabbed at the phone nearby and punched in Camee's number with shaking hands. She hadn't talked to her for weeks, but she knew Camee would listen, knew she'd pray as if she had a window into her life. Right now, Camee was her lifeline. She was desperate.

Ringing, ringing. Finally, Camee's voice.

"Camee? It's Suzy. I know it's late, but I need to talk to someone." She exhaled. Another sob escaped.

"It's OK. I was getting ready for bed, but I'm still up. What's going on?"

She breathed. Camee's voice was calm, caring. She needed that. "I have a broken light bulb." Suzy hugged her knees into her arms and against her clenching stomach. "I drew lines on my arm with it. Now I want to cut myself. The way I'm feeling, I'm afraid . . . I might do more."

She grabbed at the phone nearby and punched in Camee's number with shaking hands. She hadn't talked to her for weeks, but she knew Camee would listen.

"Suzy, I'm here. Can you tell me what you need?"

"I don't know."

But she did know some of it. She was tired of carrying around the false images and trying to live up to them. Tired of carrying around the lie she told of the "rape." She no longer knew who she was or even who she wanted to be. She and Josh were together, but she couldn't talk to him. Their relationship was mostly physical. He didn't know how badly she was struggling. No one knew. And now that she was on the phone she realized she felt too ashamed to tell Camee.

"What can I do to help you?" Camee's voice was gentle. "Do you want to talk?"

She didn't, really. "No."

"I want to pray for you. OK?"

"Yes." Suzy wanted that connection with God again. She needed it. As she huddled on the floor all she felt was the pressing darkness of choices hounding her, shaming her, convincing her she was worthless. She wanted hope again.

Camee began to pray, "God, you are not far away from Suzy . . ."

Suzy listened as her friend called out for God to protect her and shield her from anything that would harm her. She prayed for Suzy to know God's love for her, his peace. Suzy longed to know it, to feel it lift her out of the pain and loneliness. And mistakes.

Camee finished. "How're you feeling now?"

> **Suzy wanted that connection with God again. She needed it. As she huddled on the floor all she felt was the pressing darkness of choices hounding her.**

How did she feel? Talking to Camee, hearing her prayer, helped ease the anxiety a little, but was it enough? She didn't want to bother Camee any more. "This helped. Thanks."

"I'll keep praying for you, 'kay? And I'll call tomorrow and see how you're doing."

"OK. Bye."

Suzy set her phone down. Her parents were in other parts of the house, probably thinking she was asleep. Though it had lessened, her fear and anxiety left her feeling unraveled. She dropped her head back against the wall.

The light bulb was still there. Again, the craving began to nag at her. She wanted the relief the cuts would bring. And maybe more—to make *everything* stop. The shaking and the pain—her stomach stirred like a returning storm. She scooted toward the wastebasket and tipped it upward to get to the broken bulb. Tears streamed down her face. *I can't fight this.* She held the glass and rocked back against the wall. She pressed the glass against her arm but then pulled it away, held it against her ankle but pulled it away—each time almost cutting but stopping just short of it. Relentless, dark thoughts tormented her. She knew she was in trouble.

She dropped her hand to the phone again, glanced at the clock, jerked her hand away. She couldn't call. An hour had passed. Camee was asleep by now. What should she do? She couldn't go to Mom or Dad—what would they do? Ask questions? Take her somewhere? Right now, she just wanted the feelings to stop. That's all.

She picked up the phone and again called Camee.

> **Relentless, dark thoughts tormented her. She knew she was in trouble.**

Camee's mom answered. Suzy almost hung up. "Can I talk to Camee?" Would her mom let her? She felt her heart pounding, hoping.

"I'll go get her, Suzy. Hold on."

She waited, barely able to hold the phone, her anxiety intensifying.

Finally, Camee's sleepy voice. "Are you OK?"

"No, I can't stop thinking about hurting myself. I've never felt it so strong."

"OK, I'm coming over."

Suzy hung up. The broken bulb lay on the floor next to her. She grabbed a T-shirt and covered it. After what seemed like only moments had passed she heard her mother's surprised voice. Talking. Footsteps. Then Camee came through her bedroom door in pajamas, peeling off her winter coat.

She dropped her coat and knelt by Suzy. "You can make it through this. I know you can."

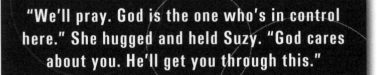

"We'll pray. God is the one who's in control here." She hugged and held Suzy. "God cares about you. He'll get you through this."

Suzy was crying and shaking. "I'm glad you're here."

"Where's the broken bulb?"

Suzy lifted a shirt next to her.

"I'm going to throw this away." Camee left the room and then came back and sat by Suzy. "My mom is talking to your mom. She said I could stay the night, but I have to go to school in the morning." She placed a hand on Suzy's arm. "I'll be here, and I won't let you hurt yourself. We'll pray. God is the one who's in control here." She hugged and held Suzy. "God cares about you. He'll get you through this."

Suzy nodded. She felt she didn't deserve God's love or rescue. She had turned her back on him and walked—no, *ran*— a different direction. Now she only knew the tangled hold of so many things on her life, wrapping around her mind, heart, and body, threatening to pull her under and carry her to some awful place of no return.

A few days later, Suzy was on the phone with Martin, her youth pastor.

"I heard you've been having a hard time."

Suzy closed her eyes and gripped the phone. "Yeah."

"A lot of people really care about you. Sharon and Karen are great ladies that you can count on to be there for you."

"I know."

Sharon was the senior pastor's wife and Karen was an elder's wife. They both often asked her how she was doing.

"We talked and Sharon has a group of women that are willing to get together with you and pray for you. When you're ready, just give me the word, and I'll call."

> She didn't need any questions right now.
> She had enough of those after the night
> Camee came over to her place.

Suzy paused. What was she supposed to say? She knew they were reaching out to her, but she felt embarrassed and ashamed. "OK, I will," she answered. "Thanks." Suzy set her phone down. It was wet with her tears.

Suzy tugged the refrigerator handle. It seemed heavy. The door released its seal and she stared at the shelves inside. Nothing looked good. She was almost too tired to eat. Her eyes shifted their focus to the cuts and scars that showed on the arm holding open the door. She closed the refrigerator and pulled her sleeve down. She didn't need any questions right now. She had enough of those after the night Camee came over to her place.

"Couldn't find anything?" Mom had come in the room carrying some dish towels. She put them away, closed some drawers, straightened things. "We have leftover pizza. How would that be?"

"No, I'm not really that hungry." Suzy leaned on the counter and dropped her chin into her propped hands.

"OK." Her mom pulled open the dishwasher and began to unload dishes. "How about some leftover chicken?"

"Mom." Suzy's voice was sharp.

"Just making a suggestion."

Mom looked hurt now. *What is her problem?*, Suzy thought, rolling her eyes and letting out an exasperated sigh. They weren't getting along lately. She reached across the counter, chose a slice of apple sitting in a dish, and nibbled at her snack. She found herself counting the number of days to Christmas break. Eleven. It would be nice if it came sooner.

She reached for another apple slice and heard a soft gasp from her mother. Suzy wrinkled her brow into an annoyed *what?*

"I don't know what to do, Suzy. What is it going to take?" She was shaking her head and staring at Suzy's arm.

Suzy looked down and saw that her sleeve had come up again. A fresh cut showed. When she raised her head Mom was at her side, grabbing her hand, and pulling her away from the counter.

six

"What are you doing, Mom?" Suzy tried to pull her arm back, but Mom only held more firmly. She didn't look angry. What was going through her mind? Where were they going? Her mom stepped through the dining room into the Pretty Room, decorated for Christmas.

Mom dropped to her knees in front of the Christmas tree, took Suzy's hands, and pulled her down to kneel next to her. Suzy felt too surprised to resist.

> **She thought her mom had lost it,
> but—whatever—she'd go along with it.**

"We're gonna pray." Mom looked determined, sad. "I know you've been close to God. You were happier before. Now you're tired a lot. You're mad at us most of the time. You're hurting yourself, and we're afraid for you." She stopped and caught her breath. "We need to pray."

She thought her mom had lost it, but—whatever—she'd go along with it. Mom bowed her head and Suzy stared at the ornaments on the tree. She listened to the quiet pleas of the prayer. It was simple, genuine. Mom cared. Dad cared too. And yet they didn't know half of what she was going through. They saw the cuts and scars on her skin, but didn't know about the cuts and scars inside her heart. Tears burned Suzy's eyes and she swallowed. Her search to belong had left her feeling lost, soiled, disconnected.

In one of the hanging balls, she caught her reflection staring back at her. Scratched. Distorted. Fitting for how she now saw herself.

SEDUCED BY SEX : SAVED BY LOVE

> For I know my transgressions,
> and my sin is always before me.
>
> PSALM 51:3

SOMEONE TO TRUST

Suzy was beginning to reach out for help. Others were reaching out to her. Was she ready to grab the lifeline yet? She wasn't sure. It meant facing things that hurt too deeply. Or hurting others deeply. It meant telling the truth when a part of her wasn't even certain what the whole truth was. And it meant letting people in. Could she trust? Just when the risk seemed possible, her guilt and shame would surge again.

She was quickly coming to the end of her resources. Later she recalled, "I was so far into the lifestyle I was giving into, I was running into exhaustion. I wanted it to end, but I didn't know how to end it."

Cutting on herself, with its numbing effect, had worked for her in the past. She wanted to turn to it again. Her self-inflicted scratch from the broken light bulb and the intensity of the emotions sent a warning—she might go too far this time. The pressure seemed menacing and dark, spiritual on the far side of evil. Destructive.

She had pushed God away, but she knew someone who hadn't. Camee. Suzy said, "Cam and I had always had a special connection from the beginning of our friendship. The way she lived out her faith made her the only friend I would turn to that horrible night."

Camee remembered the intensity of that night as well. "I had never heard of anyone cutting themselves just to cut themselves, but I thought, 'This is good that she's reaching out. Shows that she trusts me.' I really had no clue what I was getting into. But I knew it was spiritual too. I felt pretty confident in God even though I was very scared. How old was I? Maybe like sixteen, and only a few years old in the Lord."

Suzy didn't tell Camee the whole story yet. Camee noticed. "She was really quiet about who she involved," Camee recalled. "It seemed to me that the people who got involved were the ones who stepped in and said, 'OK, we recognize that something's wrong, and we're going to help you get help.'"

So much had changed in a few months. Her parents didn't understand what was happening with their daughter. "I was hurting for her," her mom, Connie, said. "When your own child is going through this, it's heartwrenching."

While Suzy was still cautious about letting people into her world, God was putting options in place for her. Others in her church, including her youth pastor, Martin, had noticed her struggle, and though Suzy's parents didn't attend the same church until later, they began to feel the support Suzy was starting to receive. Sharon, the senior pastor's wife, and Karen were two women who began to reach out to Suzy and her parents. Suzy felt alone, but she wasn't. When she was ready, they'd be there.

Sometimes all it takes is one friend, one listening ear. It's a beginning.

    SEDUCED BY SEX : SAVED BY LOVE

> Get to know the young people around you and let them know you're available if they need to talk about some of the tough stuff they're going through. Check in with them from time to time so they know your offer still stands.

FRIENDS? OR NOT?

Kaela (not a real name, but representing a real person in Suzy's life) and Camee (her real name) were opposite kinds of friends for Suzy.

Kaela was there for Suzy when she wanted to sneak out of her house, smoke, hang out with guys, drink, make out, have sex with guys. We'll give Kaela credit for rescuing Suzy from a situation that was headed in a really bad direction, the one at Nate's house, but the lifestyle they encouraged in each other by hanging out was far from great. Suzy, in fact, was choking in that lifestyle.

Camee, Suzy's other friend, was someone she could count on all the way. She accepted Suzy even at her worst, cared about her in the good times and the bad. Suzy watched her friend live above the typical teen pressures and stay steady through her faith in God. Camee didn't push that on Suzy at all, but she naturally modeled how to make good choices while living in a sex-saturated culture that throws all kinds of intense pressures at you.

Keep an eye on these two as Suzy's story continues. Just so you know, Suzy and Kaela aren't friends today. Their friendship no longer worked once Suzy started making changes in her life. Kaela wouldn't support those efforts. Camee and Suzy, on the other hand, are still great friends.

Camee recently said, "Suzy is the person I have felt most connected to over the years—that I've had the most intimate friendship with, including [being] spiritually tied together with the Lord." The two of them lost touch for a while, but then reconnected. Camee said, "I was going through a really tough spot, and Suzy walked me through that, mentoring me over the phone. We've been able to be there for each other."

A group of fourteen- to twenty-two-year-olds were asked what they *felt* should be most valued when it comes to popularity. Their answers make a great list for what creates powerful friendships. Here are some of the most-repeated items on their list:

Trustworthy	Respectful
Discerning	Has self-respect
Moral	Has willpower
Prays	Nonjudgmental
Serves others	Good listener
Honors others	Encourager
Generous	Depends on Christ
Humble	Values eternity

It may be pretty hard to find all of these characteristics in one friend, but it's not impossible to inspire all of them in each other. You'll not only be more likely to have the kind of friends that reach out when you're in trouble, but you can be that kind of friend to them as well.

SEDUCED BY SEX : SAVED BY LOVE

If you're in leadership with youth, don't ignore the fringe kids. They need you reaching out to them as much as, or more than, anyone else. One of the things they probably need most is just some guidance. Be a friend—a good friend.

OUT OF THE RUBBLE

The Bible tells the story of Rahab, a woman who lived in the city walls of Jericho, trying to make a living as an innkeeper. She also had the reputation of being a prostitute. We're not told much about those she knew, but it seems she didn't have many friends who encouraged her to live a different life. She was pretty stuck in it.

But then she saw her chance to get out of that life when two spies from the nation of Israel showed up at her inn. She protected them and snuck them out of her city, but also begged them to save her and her family when the Israelites returned to destroy the city. You can read the whole story in Joshua chapters 2 through 6, but the part to look at now is where the spies told her that when the battle began she was to stay in her house and tie a scarlet cord in her window (Joshua 2:17-21). Then she would be safe, they said.

When the Israelite army returned to attack, Jericho's walls began to crumble. Rahab believed that God would honor her symbol of trust in him. The city was destroyed, but she and her family walked away, leaving her old life in the rubble. The rest of her life she lived with the Israelites, new friends who encouraged her to grow in her faith in God. In fact, if you look in Matthew 1:5, you'll see that she became a part of the genealogy of Jesus himself.

Rahab carried the shame of a harlot but wanted a different life. She trusted God in a culture that despised him. The cord represented salvation when all was coming to ruins around her. It represented her faith and desire to turn from her old life and go to God—the one she knew she could trust to help her live differently. For us, the scarlet cord can also remind us of Jesus' blood and sacrifice, and God's love that brings us out of our rubble.

Our choices may have brought us pretty low, and we may have friends who don't mind keeping us there. But Rahab's story gives us hope. Trust God to bring you to a better place—closer to him, and to better friends who care about you.

God, I'm reaching out to you. You look deep into my life and know all that I struggle with, all that pulls me down and far away from you and your purposes for me. Help me make that steady commitment to leave behind any ways that I show my unfaithfulness to you. Show me friends who will encourage and support a stronger way of living. Help me be that kind of friend. AMEN.

**Teach me your way, O Lord,
and I will walk in your truth;
give me an undivided heart,
that I may fear your name.**

PSALM 86:11

SEDUCED BY SEX : SAVED BY LOVE

GOING DEEPER

■ A part of sticking firm with your beliefs about sex and relationships is hanging out with friends who share and support those values. Take a look again at the qualities mentioned earlier in this chapter that provide a pretty good list of what to look for in a friend. How can you work toward strengthening your friendship situation?

■ "Hanging out," for some, involves alcohol and drugs. That impairs judgment and can easily lead to sexual compromise. What plans can you put in place to be sure that you stay away from situations that will affect your judgment?

■ What are you struggling with right now? Which solid friends and support people can you turn to?

DEEPER STILL

The scarlet cord was a powerful symbol of faith for Rahab. Create or choose an object that can represent two things: your faith that God will rescue you or keep you safe from the crumbling walls of false intimacy; and your commitment to his plan for you. It can be a ring or a necklace that you wear, or something you keep in a prominent place in your room. Write out a statement of its meaning to you. Share it with a friend or support person.

seven

The Holy Spirit was totally working in me to tell the truth.
He was changing the situation from darkness to light.

SUZY SAT ON THE FLOOR in front of her full-length mirror and pulled her brush through her hair. She was too tired to care if she looked perfect—even for the day's start to the new semester. *New semester—right.* The last one had begun with so much hope; this one was drained of it. With all that she had thrown away with her choices, there was no "new" in sight.

"Only a lot of crap," she said out loud, angry with herself, weary. "And you're going to have to live with it for the rest of your life." Her eyes pooled with acid tears.

She grabbed a couple of tissues to salvage what little makeup was left. As she tossed the crumpled wad into the wastebasket, she spotted her journal on the floor, near her closet. She reached for it and began thumbing through its pages. All she found were scribbles about a life she didn't like and messed-up choices she'd erase if she could. One thing wasn't in the journal—the stupid lie about the rape. She wished it could be as absent from the last few months as it was from her journal. Fresh tears coursed down her cheeks. She picked up a pen and wrote one sentence: *God, please forgive me for telling the lie about the rape.*

She grabbed another tissue, blew her nose, and finished getting ready for school. As she stepped out of her bedroom to go to school, the journal and its plea for forgiveness remained open on the floor by her closet.

Later, Suzy returned from school, exhausted. She shifted her backpack as she came through the door. She saw her mom in the kitchen as she passed.

"Hi, Mom."

"Hi."

> She picked up a pen and wrote one sentence:
> *God, please forgive me for telling the lie about the rape.*

As she got to her room and dropped her pack to the floor, a flicker of Mom's mood registered. Her voice had sounded tired, hollow—she wasn't happy about something. Suzy shrugged. Probably nothing. She changed into her favorite baggy jeans, slipped on a sweatshirt, and flopped onto her bed. She should probably do homework, but she was too tired to think about anything right now.

Mom tapped on her door and opened it. "Suzy?"

"Yeah?"

Mom pushed the door open wider and kept her hand on the doorknob. She hesitated, seeming unsure of what she wanted to do—or say. Finally she spoke, but her words seemed tense and edged with sadness. "While you were at school I found your journal open."

Suzy shot a glance toward the spot where she had sat with her journal that morning. The small book now lay closed and placed neatly on top of her CD player. She braced for what she knew must be coming.

"I read your prayer. You lied about the rape?" Mom winced just saying it out loud.

Suzy's stomach knotted; she felt an overwhelming clash of emotions. Anger and hurt. Fear and shame. She waited to hear more.

"We suspected after you went to the hospital, but weren't sure." Her mom's hand still gripped the doorknob tightly.

Memories and conversations flashed through Suzy's mind. Deep inside she had sensed they guessed the truth. "Does Dad know you read my journal?"

Finally she spoke, but her words seemed tense and edged with sadness. "While you were at school I found your journal open."

"Yes." Mom stood silent, seeming to have run out of words. Suzy had none herself.

Her mom turned and closed her door. Suzy wrapped her arms around herself and let her tears wash through in waves. She had put her parents through so much; this was just one more thing. And yet, the tears that freely flowed also came from a sense of relief. One less way she needed to pretend.

Finally, the tide of tears receded and she took a quivering breath. She knew Dad was home by now. She'd go talk to him. She stood, wiped the tears with the back of her sleeve, and opened her door. The house was quiet. She walked toward the front of the house and found him in the Pretty Room. The TV was on. He seemed to be looking through it.

seven

"Dad?" Suzy stood just inside the entry.

He looked up at her, the hurt in his eyes unmistakable.

"Mom told me you know about the lie."

He nodded. He looked ready to cry, weary.

She couldn't hold back her tears. "I'm so sorry."

He didn't say anything. She didn't expect it. What *could* he say? He had thought his daughter was raped, and then, like Mom, had doubted it but wondered why she'd lie and then keep it going for so long. So much of her life was a mess and a lie—where would she have begun? She had let him down big time, even more than he knew. She couldn't imagine his face if he knew about the guys she'd been with. The guilt she felt from those choices clung to her like dirty sludge. Could he see it?

> **And yet, the tears that freely flowed also came from a sense of relief. One less way she needed to pretend.**

She wanted to go to him, hug him. She wanted to become Daddy's little girl again. But she couldn't.

She turned and walked away.

A few days later Suzy was at a youth club retreat on the Oregon coast, still heavy at heart. She zipped open her duffle bag in the room she'd share with Camee and two others. Earlier, the group, about forty students, had piled into cars and headed to the beach. Suzy and the others spent the chilly winter afternoon jumping off sandy dunes, wading in the edges of the water, just hanging out.

SEDUCED BY SEX : SAVED BY LOVE

She'd tried to laugh, tried to have fun. At certain moments, she almost felt like the old Suzy again. Almost. But so much was different. So much was changed, lost. The weight of her compromises and the lie was never far from her mind.

> She wanted to go to him, hug him. She wanted to become Daddy's little girl again. But she couldn't. She turned and walked away.

Tears hovered close to the surface and now burned as she pulled her pajamas out of her bag.

"It's so cool we got in the same room," Camee said as she dug into her bag.

"Yeah, I'm really glad." Suzy smiled at her friend. Since her parents found her journal, she wanted others to know the truth. It would be hard, but if there was one good person to start with, it would be Camee. Could she tell her? She dropped her bag to the floor and sat cross-legged on her bed.

Camee joined her. "Wasn't the beach fun? But cold." She gave a mock shiver.

For the next few moments the two of them laughed at some of the stuff the guys had done and giggled at discovering they both wore glow-in-the-dark Band-Aids from the cuts they got that day. The other two girls in the room rolled their eyes and crawled into their beds. Suzy and Camee tried harder to be quiet.

Finally, when Suzy was sure their roommates were asleep, she got serious again. "Camee, I need to tell you something," she whispered.

"OK," Camee whispered back. She looked expectant, her smile dropping as if she sensed Suzy's seriousness.

> **Finally, when Suzy was sure their roommates were asleep, she got serious again. "Camee, I need to tell you something," she whispered.**

"Remember at the beginning of the school year when I said I got raped?"

"Yeah."

"It was a lie."

"It was?" Camee sat forward, dropping her hands on Suzy's knees.

The tears came quick. "I know I shouldn't have done it." Suzy poured out the whole story about how the lie began. "After I told it, I just went with it. It seemed to work. I thought it explained the cuts. Then I just wanted it to go away. I didn't know what to do when it spread. I started telling it myself, almost believing it was true."

"I know. I heard it from you. Does anyone else know it's a lie?"

"My mom found out for sure when she read my journal, and she told my dad." Recalling her mom's sadness and her father's hurt expression brought new tears.

"She read your journal?"

"I guess I left it open when I went to school that day. I didn't do it on purpose, but I'm glad it happened. I've wanted the lie to be over for a long time. I just didn't know how."

"What'd your parents do?"

"I wish they'd grounded me or something, but they didn't do anything. That's almost worse. They just seem . . . really sad. I've put them through a lot lately."

Suzy began to sob.

Camee put her arms around her. "You're telling the truth. That's an awesome start."

"Yeah. I want it to be over." She knew there was a lot more truth to tell before that happened. Suzy caught her breath and let the sobs slow. "I shouldn't have lied. People are going to hate me when they find out."

"Who else are you going to tell?"

"I want to tell some of my other friends here in the group. But not here. Not this weekend."

Camee put her arms around her.
"You're telling the truth.
That's an awesome start."

"Awesome. You're trying to make it right. I bet the angels are rejoicing because you've confessed this. Can you imagine that?"

Suzy shook her head. "Not really. Wish I could."

Camee grew excited. "Hey, let's ask God what they're singing." She seemed to want to cheer Suzy up.

She looked at her friend's face to see if Camee was for real. "Are you kidding?" She laughed and rubbed away some of her tears.

Maybe God *would* forgive her. She didn't know how she was going to get out of the rest of her mess, but for this moment she felt hope.

"No." Camee bowed her head and prayed, thanking God for Suzy's confession. ". . . And God, if the angels are singing, tell us what song so we can sing it too." She looked up at Suzy. "Well? What do you think they're singing? I think it's—"

"Sing Hallelujah to the Lord," both girls said together, then laughed. They looked at their roommates' beds. They hadn't woken them.

Another rush of tears filled Suzy's eyes. She quieted her voice. "I can't believe we thought of the same song. Let's sing it."

Coming up with the song together, Suzy felt the angels must be singing too. Maybe God *would* forgive her. She didn't know how she was going to get out of the rest of her mess, but for this moment she felt hope.

> What this adds up to, then, is this: no more lies,
> no more pretense. Tell your neighbor the truth.
> In Christ's body we're all connected to each other, after all.
> When you lie to others, you end up lying to yourself.
> EPHESIANS 4:25 (THE MESSAGE)

More Confession

A lie settles in and festers. It never feels right. Never feels good.

Suzy wanted to get rid of her lies. The first one she tackled was the lie about the rape that never happened. She said, "There were no options left. I couldn't continue living the lie anymore. It went so against the grain. I just couldn't do it anymore."

Not surprisingly, Suzy got different reactions to telling the truth. It affected her parents on a deeper level, so in them she saw sadness and disappointment. Suzy read her Dad's response as "I'm done with you."

When asked what he felt that day, Don, Suzy's father, said, "Well, you know I was very sad that I had failed her." He blamed himself as a workaholic. "I could have spent more time with her," he said. "I think it would have changed things. When you spend more time with kids they learn things, more gets discussed."

A few weeks after the beach retreat, Suzy, with Camee's encouragement, confessed the lie to a group of her friends at a youth club meeting. Sobbing, she told them she was sorry for having broken their trust. Many hugged her afterward and told her they were glad she hadn't been raped. Some challenged her faith. A few days later, while walking through her school parking lot, one girl, who was like a big sister to Suzy, told her, "You know, being a Christian is not a joke." Looking back, Suzy said, "It was tough love. She wasn't being mean or anything. It was true. It's not a joke—to God or anybody."

The truth about the rape was out and she felt the relief. "The Holy Spirit was totally working in me to tell the truth, changing the situation from darkness to light," Suzy said.

But other lies, not as easy to shake, still clung. About the image she had been trying to build, trying it on like a new outfit, she said, "I had a hard time taking off the jacket. I couldn't just put it down. I had become that person so much." When asked what she thought about *that* Suzy, she said, "She was scary. She would do anything to get someone's approval, including harm herself, and she was physically harming herself. She didn't stand on anything. For the sake of acceptance, she'd do anything. That's dangerous—really dangerous."

She saw how easily she left God out of the picture. "I was so immature and naive, I don't think anything anyone would have told me would have stopped me from pushing forward with the rebelliousness toward God and the destructiveness toward my body."

Suzy felt she had stretched God's grace as far as it would go. She said she was "afraid to be in the same room with him." And though she needed to learn to take God seriously, she'd soon discover she didn't have to run from him.

Become a better listener to the teens you know. Listen attentively to what they say, but also tune into what's behind their words. Listen without jumping to conclusions or judgments and without giving immediate advice.

SEDUCED BY SEX : SAVED BY LOVE

Suzy took a step. She had many more to take, but it was a start. Are you living a lie that you need to get out of? Here are some lies that others have believed:

> "At the time I thought I was doing the right thing to have sex whenever. I was going along with the crowd."

> "I believed premarital sex was fun and made you feel wanted. That's a lie I was fed. I lived it and it became destructive."

> "My core belief was, 'To be a man you gotta get some.'"

> "I was told that giving my body equaled getting love in return. I was hungry for attention and love."

> "I received my beliefs from molesters—'I am only good for sex. I am only a body.'"

> "The music I listened to convinced me that premarital sex is not wrong, but normal and fun."

> "I learned from my dad that I had no right to say no, that men were allowed to do and say whatever they wanted to me, and I was supposed to keep quiet through it."

> "I've come a long way from just being, like, 'Oh, just some girl, I don't care.'"

> "All of the abuse left me with the thought that I was created to be abused—that's what I was here for."

> "I was like, 'If I have sex, I have sex. I don't care.' What was the big deal?"

Each of these individuals realized the destructive message behind what they had believed. They're taking steps toward getting a different message into their hearts and minds. You probably have a pretty good idea of some of the lies you've believed and lived out. See them for what they are. Tell yourself the truth. Tell someone else. Tell God.

> If you see someone acting out through risky sexual behavior or in other ways, consider the possibility that they might be living with some lies they believe about themselves. Build relationships that provide opportunities to talk on a deeper level.

WAITING FOR YOU

If you've been believing or living a lie, you have another option.

You've probably heard the story Jesus told about the son who asked for his inheritance even before his father had died, received it—and then left his family. You can read the whole parable in Luke 15:11-32. This guy did it all—spent his money and indulged in drinking, parties, and sex—until he had nothing left. The only job he could get was feeding pigs. He had a huge wake-up call at a moment when he was so hungry he was ready to eat the pig slop. He had believed lots of lies about "the good life." Look where it landed him—in some pretty serious muck.

He decided he wanted to get out of there—and not just because it wasn't fun feeding pigs. He knew he'd blown it with his choices and wanted to get away from that kind of life. He didn't feel he deserved to be a son, but maybe his dad would take him as a servant. He would go back home and ask his father's forgiveness.

Many dads would have given up looking for their son, gone on with life the best they could. But there's something really cool about this story. Luke 15:20 says, "But while he was still a long way off, his father saw him and was filled with compassion for him; he ran to his son, threw his arms around him and kissed him."

As the son got closer to his old home, the road wasn't empty. The father was on that road, as he had been every day since his son left, watching for his return. With some dads, that might be scary. This one saw his son, ran to him, wrapped his arms around him, and kissed him. When his son came home, Dad received him with open arms.

In the same way, you, God's child, may have believed lies, may have blown it big time and been sucked in to some way of living that is far from what he intended for you. Get away from those things that mess up your life and mess with your mind. Go back to your Father, God. He's waiting with open arms.

God, when I'm really honest with myself I see the ways I'm living in the muck and far from what you had in mind for me. I can see some of the lies I've believed. Help me each day to see any lie that keeps me trapped in a lifestyle that distorts my view of sex and relationships. Show me the amazing truth of who I can be and the purposes you have for my life. Forgive me for living the lies, for treating others and myself in really messed-up ways. I want to come home to you. AMEN.

> But now in Christ Jesus you who once were far away
> have been brought near through the blood of Christ.
>
> EPHESIANS 2:13

GOING DEEPER

■ Sometimes we have to slow down to really see the lies we are living out. (Like, "That music, or that website, is OK for me.") Take a moment to look closely at your own life and the ways you're living out your values about sex and relationships. What do you need to tackle?

■ Are you off track with your life? When you think about the story Jesus told in Luke 15, how do you view your road back? What are some specific steps you can take?

■ Shame and guilt can keep us stuck where we are. Are there ways your view of God might be keeping you from seeing him waiting for you with open arms?

DEEPER STILL

In thirty seconds, write down short phrases depicting what you think about yourself. Another thirty seconds—what you believe about sex and relationships. Thirty more—God's view of who you are. Thirty more—God's view of sex and relationships. Now cross out the lies and circle the truths. Ask a wise, older person or pastor to help you identify the truths and live them out.

eight

*I was a black hole and just so corroded with choices I had made
and the determination to be different instead of obedient.
There was no relationship with my parents at that point.*

"THEY'RE JUST CIGARETTES." Suzy turned away and rubbed the towel harder through her wet hair. Standing in her parents' bathroom, she could see her mom's expression in the mirror, and it was way more steamed than the glass was.

"I thought you quit."

"I didn't."

"I see that. I found these in your armoire." Her mom was holding four cigarettes in the palm of her hand.

Suzy didn't answer. What was Mom's problem? *She* smoked.

Mom sighed, her voice softening a level, exasperation replacing anger. "I'm taking these away. We'll talk about this more when you get home from school." She left the room. Suzy stared after her and let the meaning of her mom's words sink in.

Great. That means Dad is going to get involved. She jerked her towel off her hair and threw it to the floor. What was Mom doing in her stuff anyway? Parents—what a pain. Then dread settled in. The last thing she wanted was an after-school, parent-teen session on smoking.

Well, forget you. I don't have to be around you guys anymore.

After school, she and Josh were hanging out at Nate's. She decided she wasn't going home. She had told him Kaela's plan for hiding her.

"You were going to stay in Kaela's boat?" Josh dropped his head back against the couch and laughed.

Suzy shoved his arm. "It's not funny. It was just an idea. I knew it wouldn't work. Kaela's will be the first place my parents will look." She smiled. "You have to admit hiding in the boat was creative."

He slipped his arm around her and turned back toward the TV. "So you're going to stay away for how long?"

"I don't know. I don't want to think about it right now." It was already late, far past the time her parents would have expected her home.

"We can stay here. Just don't make a big deal about it. Nate's mom won't notice."

> **She decided she wasn't going home.
> She had told him Kaela's plan for hiding her.**

The two watched TV. Nate and his mom went in and out, stopping to watch TV, getting up for food, going to other parts of the house. No one paid much attention to Suzy and Josh when they wandered back to Nate's bedroom. Once there, they kissed, then allowed their hands to wander, then moved into doing everything short of intercourse. At one point, Suzy pulled back. Josh got frustrated, an undertone of anger in his words. "Hey, didn't your parents teach you to finish what you started?"

SEDUCED BY SEX : SAVED BY LOVE

No, they hadn't taught her any of this. She sat up on the edge of the bed. What was she doing? Sometimes she felt good in Josh's arms. He seemed to care about her, but it seemed like their whole relationship was about sex. She was getting sick of it. Sick of herself. It left her feeling empty, though she wasn't sure why, given all the talk about how great it was supposed to be. For now she just wanted to get through this night and figure out what she was going to do the next day.

> **No one paid much attention to Suzy and Josh when they wandered back to Nate's bedroom. Once there, they kissed, then allowed their hands to wander.**

As she pulled on her clothes, she noticed car lights slowly passing. She knelt by the window and inched open the curtain. *Yep, Mom and Dad's car.* She dropped the curtain back in place. *They won't look here. They don't even know Nate, don't even know I hang out here sometimes.*

In the middle of the night, Suzy woke up in Josh's arms. All three of them were sleeping in Nate's room: Nate in his bed, Suzy and Josh on the floor on a blanket. She thought of her parents and what they must be thinking. They probably thought she was with a friend. She yawned and fell back asleep.

In the morning, she and Josh walked to his house. It was a school day, but she was skipping it, and Josh didn't go to public school. Maybe he did school at home or something. She never asked. They really didn't spend a lot of time talking, so she didn't know a lot about him. Come to think of it, he never asked much about her either.

As they stepped in the door, Josh's dad laid into him. Suzy slipped away to the bathroom. When she came out, Josh was alone, rummaging through the refrigerator.

"Everything OK?" Suzy leaned her elbows on the counter and watched him pull out a jug of milk.

"Yeah, just my dad—always pissed about something." He set the milk on the counter. "Want some cereal?"

"Sure."

Suzy stayed through the morning and into the afternoon. Waves of anxiety began to hit when she'd think about what she would do next. She'd shut it down with anger—who cared what her parents thought?—then the anxiety would return.

They passed the time watching TV and making out. Not much conversation, just a lot of lip-to-lip contact. Then more.

> **They really didn't spend a lot of time talking, so she didn't know a lot about him. Come to think of it, he never asked much about her either.**

With the TV blaring, the clothes came off, and the making-out escalated to sex.

Thoughts, warnings, and accusations punched through her mind.

How many times is this now, Suzy—nine, ten, twelve? Or have you lost count? . . . Her self-talk continued. *What am I doing anyway?*

Living like this will only end up in a lot of hurt. It's about more than pregnancy or STDs. What am I doing to myself? To my soul?

Soul? She'd slapped God in the face with her choices, expecting his grace would always be there. She'd taken it too far. He'd never want her back.

She felt the growing battle in her heart. She didn't want this life, but how could it be different? She dressed again and felt like she was stepping into more shame, pulling guilt over her head and onto her shoulders. She didn't want to face her parents, but their deal about smoking was nothing compared to this—nothing.

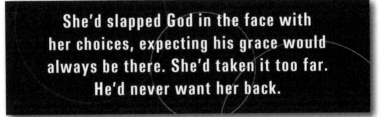

She'd slapped God in the face with her choices, expecting his grace would always be there. She'd taken it too far. He'd never want her back.

Kaela called. Suzy's parents were coming to pick her up, so she needed to get over there.

When Suzy's parents picked her up from Kaela's, they didn't say a word. They had no idea what she'd been doing, but she could feel their disappointment, their sadness. They didn't know what to do with her. She didn't know either, but she was tired of it all. Maybe more than they were.

> You're addicted to thrills? What an empty life!
> The pursuit of pleasure is never satisfied.
>
> PROVERBS 21:17 (THE MESSAGE)

ON EMPTY

Suzy had come to the end of herself. Narrowing the sex to one relationship seemed like it would help, but it didn't. Her dream to be someone special had been marred by a false ideal she pulled from the pages of the world. Things still felt off. Empty.

"I didn't know what I was doing," she recalled later. "It was beyond me that I could have a meaningful relationship. I was caught up in doing what I thought was expected of me." And, caught up, she had no way to think differently about herself and relationships. She said, "I was dry, and in my mind I had done it all. There was just no way out that I knew of—until later when I was in a repentant place."

CROSSING THE LINE

Suzy felt she had done it all. She had no more boundaries when it came to sex. Not only was none of it a big deal, it had no meaning for her.

Boundaries get crossed. It's even worse when boundaries really haven't been defined. Suzy walked into her first sexual experience with Matt having heard the message that it's God's plan to save sex for marriage. But *hearing* a message doesn't mean you'll follow it.

There's a lot of confusion about where the lines of compromise should be drawn. And once you start crossing whatever lines you've set, it's hard to go back.

Some junior highers to early twenties interviewed for this book shared their definitions of sexual compromise—where crossing the line was for them:

> "Sexual stuff is OK, but only have sex when you truly love your partner"
>
> "Viewing sexually explicit/revealing images of women intentionally"
>
> "Midnight backseat grope-fest"
>
> "Letting a boy totally feel me up and too much touching in certain areas"
>
> "Nothing below the belt"
>
> "Having sexual intercourse"
>
> "Any sexual touching that may lead to sex"
>
> "Oral or traditional (sex). Everything up to that point I'm OK with—if I love the person"
>
> "Taking off the clothes"
>
> "Something you could not do in front of your parents"
>
> "Going all the way"
>
> "I wouldn't know because I've never been close to a guy. But if he starts touching me in wrong places, that would be 'crossing the line'"

Most said they believed sex was reserved for marriage, but look closely at where some of the "lines" are drawn. For some, before even reaching their line, a relationship of a sexual nature has already happened.

eight

Really, defining our own line doesn't work. We too easily move it, erase it, or justify why we crossed it. But God gives us a really clear line. First Timothy 5:1, 2, tells us to treat those of the opposite sex "with absolute purity." First Peter 2:11 says "to abstain from sinful desires, which war against your soul."

That's just two of the many principles God has given to define the line. And he defines it because he loves us. Deeply.

> Keep the dialogue going in the groups you meet with. Know where your students stand. Talk about where the lines of commitment are and how to avoid compromise. Study Scriptures together on the subjects of sex and temptation, and discuss how to stay strong and focused with God's help.

ABSTINENCE—MORE THAN AN OPTION

So what about abstinence?

The basic definition of *abstinence* that you've probably heard is that it's an alternative to birth control or condoms, and that it allows a person to avoid STDs and pregnancy. At a basic level, abstinence is "avoiding sexual intercourse"—that's it. But here are a few of the core messages of some abstinence educators who know there's a lot more to it:

Aaron Chidester, a California Bay Area youth pastor who speaks on abstinence in church and educational settings:

"Abstinence is not about a line that you cross; it's about the direction that you're going. It's about a daily decision that takes you toward God's picture of purity. Rather than taking the mentality of 'How close can I get to the line?', take the mentality of 'How close can I get to God?'"

Garth Heckman, Black and White Productions—an organization that gives values-based presentations to schools and businesses:

"We believe that intimate touching, or anything that might induce erotic toxins in the brain, is inappropriate until marriage. Erotic toxins are simply the toxins that are released as a chemical that gives you that high, whether that might be through touching, kissing, mutual masturbation, or intercourse. So we believe the best sex is saved until marriage, and abstinence the only choice until marriage."

Barbara Wilson, abstinence educator and author of *The Invisible Bond*:

Sex, she says, is "intensely bonding . . . a mystery . . . and holy. . . . God designed sex for a husband and wife only within marriage." Hebrews 13:4 is one Scripture that teaches God's view in this way in stark, plain terms, Wilson says.

So abstinence is about a lot more than just "abstaining." In fact, it really becomes just another option that you can take or leave unless you embrace a reason to be personally committed to it. It won't matter if you *hear* that it's important to stay pure, that you can avoid negative consequences, or that you can save yourself for one partner—if you don't *get* the deeper picture of what God has in mind.

Take time to read through 1 Corinthians 6:9-20. It would probably be good to study through it in more than one version of the Bible. But here are some of the main points as paraphrased in The Message:

"Since we want to become spiritually one with the Master, we must not pursue the kind of sex that avoids commitment and intimacy, leaving us more lonely than ever—the kind of sex that can never 'become one.' . . . In sexual sin we violate the sacredness of our own bodies, these bodies that were made for God-given and God-modeled love, for 'becoming one' with another. Or didn't you realize that your body is a sacred place, the place of the Holy Spirit? Don't you see that you can't live however you please, squandering what God paid such a high price for? . . . God owns the whole works. So let people see God in and through your body" (vv. 17-20, The Message).

"Abstinence" and "saving sex until marriage" are about not violating the sacredness of God's design. They're about honoring that sacredness: honoring God . . . honoring who he created you to be . . . honoring the other person . . . and honoring his gift of "becoming one" by waiting for the right time.

If we don't get that in a deeply committed way, none of the benefits of abstinence or purity will cross our minds in the heat of the moment, when hormones and passions are raging, when we feel we're in love and sex seems so right. First Corinthians 6 calls this being mastered—as a slave is—to our whims (v. 12). The line of commitment so easily shifts.

Kevin and Amanda met when he was twenty and she was seventeen. They were each committed to staying pure for their future spouse. Kevin had had sex before, but when he met Amanda he was a new Christian and agreed that waiting for sex for marriage was the way to go.

As a child, Amanda was exposed to pornography from magazines that were given to her brother by the neighborhood "grandpa," but she grew up in a Christian home and had a strong sense of what was right and wrong. As a teen she helped with a crisis pregnancy center, and by seventeen she was one of the counselors who talked with teens who had become pregnant. Amanda saw the consequences of premarital sex firsthand. She didn't want that to happen to her. But beyond that, solid reasons for avoiding premarital sex weren't rooted in her mind and heart. Before Kevin, she had one date and one kiss, but that stirred strong emotions in her. The earlier pornography exposure played a role in intensifying the sexual feelings and temptations.

So when she and Kevin started dating, with his fairly new commitment to God and her discovery of sexual feelings, their relationship quickly gravitated toward—you guessed it—sex. When family and other adults heard about it and reacted, Kevin and Amanda felt shamed and rejected by their Christian community. Over the next year, Amanda moved in and out of her relationship with Kevin and began having sex with other guys. At times she and Kevin would come back together. One of those times, she got pregnant. Their lines of commitment had not only shifted, they were left far behind, in the dust.

Dust. Speaking of it, let's go back to the beginning, when God took the very dirt of the ground and created man. That's where you get a picture of God's original and amazing intention for sex.

> "No condom will protect your heart" is a saying that Amanda heard—and relayed to others—at the pregnancy center where she worked. Discuss *all* the consequences of premarital sex with those you lead—physical, emotional, and spiritual.

RECLAIMING THE GIFT

Look closely at the first two chapters in Genesis. God made Adam and then he created Eve—two human beings created for *each other* and no one else. And he created them with everything they needed—spiritually, emotionally, and physically—to enjoy an intimate relationship with each other . . . and no one else. They were given a gift, the freedom to enjoy getting to know each other on every level in unashamed nakedness. There was no need for a marriage contract to begin their relationship or to keep it faithful. It just was. They knew true intimacy in its purest sense—a mysterious union that God himself described as "one flesh." Theirs was not just a physical union but also a spiritual and emotional union, designed to never be broken.

But Genesis 3 describes a spiraling downward of two people as God's enemy, Satan, introduced lies, distortions, and shame to Adam and Eve's world. Wooed by this enemy, the man and the woman made choices that brought about the death of the beauty and purity that God had created in the world. Sin now blackened everything, including intimacy. Nakedness became shameful. Sex as God intended it— sacred and beautiful—became distorted. It continues to be to

SEDUCED BY SEX : SAVED BY LOVE

this day. And to this day, there is a battle to restore it. Each person, aware or not, chooses whether they will reclaim God's original sacred design.

So our decision about when and with whom we have sex goes far beyond a choice to simply stay away from it until marriage. It's a *reclaiming* choice, involving a commitment to the mysterious depth of sexual intimacy as it was designed. Reclaim true intimacy. Save it for that one person—your Eve or your Adam.

God, it's hard for me to take in all that you had planned for sexual intimacy, but help me grasp a clearer picture of your original sacred design and hold on to it. Show me how my ideas might be distorted, how my lines of commitment might be in danger of shifting. I can easily fall, as Adam and Eve did, but with you I can make the choice to reclaim all that you intended for me for true intimacy. I will trust you each day with all that I think, feel, and need. Help me stay close to you on this journey. AMEN.

Let us behave decently, as in the daytime, not in orgies and drunkenness, not in sexual immorality and debauchery, not in dissension and jealousy. Rather, clothe yourselves with the Lord Jesus Christ, and do not think about how to gratify the desires of the sinful nature.

ROMANS 13:13, 14

GOING DEEPER

■ Look again at the list of sexual boundary lines given by others in this chapter. What are the possible dangers for sexual compromise?

■ Think about your definition of sexual compromise—where crossing the line has been for you. What do you need to do to shift your line to God's standard and firmly anchor it there?

■ A false security in what we think we know or believe about sex might land us in a situation like that of Kevin and Amanda's. Are there questions you need answers to so you can make a solid commitment to God's design for sex? If yes, what are they? How you will go after them?

DEEPER STILL

Reclaim true intimacy. Choose a friend, mentor, or pastor—make sure it's someone of the same sex—who understands God's original design for sexual relations. Pray together as you reclaim and commit to true intimacy. Ask that person to hold you accountable.

If you'd like, keep a small box of fine dirt—almost like dust—to remind you of God's original plan, when he made Adam and Eve.

SEDUCED BY SEX : SAVED BY LOVE

nine

*That meeting was the beginning of me looking into
another person's eyes again.*

SUZY SHUFFLED UP TO THE ENTRANCE of the church. Briefly, she caught a glimpse of her reflection as she opened the door—sweats, no makeup. She looked plain, starkly plain, but that was just fine. It was time to strip away all pretenses. She felt exhausted and willed herself to take each step. Not only into the church—into each new moment.

Once in the lobby, she turned left into the hallway. The women who would pray for her would be waiting in Martin's office. The hallway felt long. Sadness and hopelessness clung like a dark fog. *Will this really make any difference?* She passed the copy room on the left. The self-hatred was so strong, it threatened to turn her back. Why should anyone care about her, especially after all she'd done? Why should God? She passed the senior pastor's office on the right, then the secretary's, then finally came to Martin's.

> **The self-hatred was so strong,
> it threatened to turn her back.
> Why should anyone care about her?**

"Hi, Suzy." Martin put a tentative hand on her shoulder. "You know Sharon and Karen, of course. This is Luanne and

Cetina. Why don't we have a seat? I'll pray for this time to get started, but I'm going to leave and let you talk with these women for the rest of the time."

Martin prayed and then left. Suzy felt so heavy and tired. She wanted this to work. She wasn't sure it would. God saw her in all her sludgy ugliness, and he knew how she had set him aside. But maybe his grace really was sufficient, even for her.

As they got started, she heard that message from the four women. Christ's love, his mercy, his sufficient grace. Could she turn back to him? Bring her sins to him for his forgiveness? So many of the choices she had made, she knew, had hurt her parents, hurt her, hurt God. She admitted to the lies she was a part of, the self-injury that she used to help her feel in control, the sex that spun her into a destructive lifestyle. She felt like a black bowl of muck sitting before them.

Karen prayed for her—that God would protect her and keep her from relationships that would lead her away from him. That he'd remind her of his love and his power. That she'd know that he could accomplish all that concerns her, know that he could change her heart—not by her strength, but his.

> **Christ's love, his mercy, his sufficient grace.**
> **Could she turn back to him?**
> **Bring her sins to him for his forgiveness?**

Suzy listened to the words and began to open her heart. She felt the truth of Karen's prayer, hoped that it would reach deep within her and begin real change.

More prayers reminded her who she was and could be in Christ. She was loved, forgiven, accepted as his child. She longed to believe that. Her beginning faith in him in seventh grade was so long ago, so young and sincere, but so incomplete. She easily walked into the traps ahead. Now she needed to move into something more solid to stand with against the storms she faced, and against the ones that were ahead.

> She was passionate but not condemning.
> "It's a huge loss that you've let that go."

The women encouraged her as she explained the many painful situations and choices in her life, even going back to her childhood. She wanted it all out. Over and over they led her in prayer.

"And—" she sighed and hesitated before going on. "I've been involved in a lot of sexual compromise—I've done it all."

Sharon leaned forward. "Suzy, do you understand how precious you are? How precious your body is, your virginity?" She was passionate but not condemning. "It's a huge loss that you've let that go."

"What do you mean?" Suzy felt conflicted. She knew the awfulness of the compromises. She even felt a sense of throwing herself away. But loss of virginity? Why was that important?

In the next few moments the women shared how God saw her as precious and valuable, how he gave the gift of sex for her and her future husband, but she had given that away. Once again, Suzy didn't feel their condemnation—just a hope for something more for her. She felt how sad God must be that she treated herself and his gift as if none of it were precious. She began to feel what a loss it really was. And yet it also felt like another reason to hate this Suzy she had become.

Panic pricked at Suzy. "With everyone here?"
She looked toward Sharon and Karen.
They might know some of the guys.
She felt too exposed.

She grew quiet. "What can I do?"

Luanne spoke up. "We can pray specifically about those compromises," she said.

Panic pricked at Suzy. "With everyone here?" She looked toward Sharon and Karen. They might know some of the guys. She felt too exposed.

"Or if you'd like, just with me," Luanne offered.

Suzy sighed in relief. Luanne was from another town and didn't know her family or the guys. "That would be good," Suzy said.

The other women went into the hallway, offering to continue to pray as she talked alone with Luanne. The door closed, and with her head down, the pain of her choices gripped her stomach. She told Luanne about each of the times she had sex. She felt almost detached—robotic—as she relayed each instance. Her first time in the garage with Matt. The parties and hook-ups with guys. That awful time with the guys at Nate's. Her relationship with Josh, so focused on sex. Together they prayed, Suzy letting each one go in her pleas for forgiveness.

When they finished, the other women joined them again. They taught Suzy, encouraged her, prayed with her. Hours passed. Suzy felt drained, but it was different from the exhaustion that cloaked her when she first arrived. Peace began to pour into the dry cracks of her heart.

They stood and sang songs to God, thanking him and praising him for who he is and what he had done that day. They gave Scriptures to Suzy to pray. Finally, she felt an unexpected lightness. Hope was there in her heart again. God would work in her and bring his plan for her back into place. She read one of the Scriptures that gave her that hope: "'This is what the Sovereign Lord says: On the day I cleanse you from all your sins, I will resettle your towns, and the ruins will be rebuilt. The desolate land will be cultivated instead of lying desolate in the sight of all who pass through it'" (Ezekiel 36:33-34). God had already begun that rebuilding. She could feel it.

> **Suzy felt drained, but it was different from the exhaustion that cloaked her when she first arrived. Peace began to pour into the dry cracks of her heart.**

Sharon drove Suzy home, and when she walked in the door she greeted Mom with a smile.

Mom stared at her with surprise. "You look different . . . happy."

"I am." She felt it to her core. The darkness and shame she had carried had been brought into the open and was replaced by a light that now shone through her eyes. She thought the battles must finally be over.

Suzy returned to school, only to face the pressures again. Schoolwork remained difficult. She still felt the contrast in what was popular and not popular and wished she knew how to fit in without giving up what she'd gained. Few understood or believed her changed heart. Her reputation clung; there seemed no way for it to go away.

"Look what I've got," a guy said one day, loud enough to draw attention.

Everyone turned. He pulled a bra out of his coat, held it up, and with a smirk looked straight at Suzy.

A night flashed through her mind. Just a one-time thing with this guy—before Josh. How'd he keep her bra without her realizing it?

She felt sick. She wasn't ready for this.

But he said to me, "My grace is sufficient for you, for my power is made perfect in weakness." Therefore I will boast all the more gladly about my weaknesses, so that Christ's power may rest on me.

2 CORINTHIANS 12:9

SEDUCED BY SEX : SAVED BY LOVE

Exhausted. Broken. Empty.

Choice by choice, Suzy had replaced who God had created her to be with an illusion—someone she thought others would most accept. In the process, she lost herself and didn't know how to find her way back.

"I was done," she recalled later. "I had nothing left in me. I hated myself to no end. I hated everything I had become, and I just wanted free. And I knew at that point that it was a spiritual battle, but I didn't know how to fight it."

She came to the church that day full of shame and feeling like that meeting was her last chance. "I was closed and hurting. I needed help and I knew it. And I knew that only the power of God could do it."

She entered that prayer time with women who knew her and strangers who didn't, but each of them cared deeply about her. They would spend hours praying for her, going to battle on her behalf. For part of that time, Suzy talked to them about the many things she had done. It was a safe place to bring it all out before them and before God—to confess. She said, "It's hard to explain it unless you live it, unfortunately, but there's this huge power in confession. Because you're bringing darkness into light."

In the process she began to know the deep forgiveness she ached for, the mercy and love of God covering her shame and guilt. She began to grasp what Jesus accomplished on the cross for her—his agony, his sacrifice, his death. He accepted her when all she could bring was a life stained by choices that were far from his purposes for her.

She said, "I kind of felt it was the end-all, a needed step, and I couldn't go forward without it. It was kind of like a baptism—like, 'Wash me clean.'"

Around this time, Karen, one of the women who prayed that day, often wrote about Suzy in her journals. Karen said, "I remember praying with her, and from my journals I was struggling to not lose hope. I really cared a lot about her. I would say of all the kids in the youth group, I had the most invested in her." Weeks of journal entries expressed prayers that Suzy would be willing to come and ask for help. When she did, Karen's next journal entry said, "Last night we met . . . to pray for Suzy. We met for five and a half hours. It was amazing to feel your sustaining power . . . I'm overflowing with praise and peace. Thank you."

Sharon added, "She finally understood the grace of Christ, finally understood the freedom that she could really put all that junk behind her and receive the freedom in Christ. We were all rejoicing."

Sharon drove Suzy home that night after their prayer. She remembered Suzy's changed countenance. "She was so excited that when I walked into the kitchen with her and tried to explain to her parents in just a few sentences what had happened, they were just dumbstruck. They had seen this hopeless child leave and six hours later come home this happy, incredibly joyful child."

It was a turning point for Suzy. For the first time, she began to see that though she had turned her back on God, he hadn't stopped pursuing her. She'd need that continued reminder. The shame she felt still haunted her. Her friends at school thought she was the same Suzy, and she had to face their expectations and their taunts. The fear of that would nearly destroy her.

> When someone is making changes in their life, it can be tough to face the old crowd. Be available to offer support and encouragement as well as opportunities to talk through strategies. Pray together often.

INTO HIS ARMS

Suzy felt it. God's pursuit of her. The call to something more. Hope through a cleansing. A fresh start.

God offers that to each of us. Here are a few that shared some of the steps of their journeys out of false intimacy:

Christine—on multiple sexual partners:

"I've engaged in every kind of sexual activity. I feel like my heart is scattered throughout California. I would still be living in misery and brokenness every day if it weren't for God. He saved me, literally. My choice to face everything and begin healing was very scary. I was only able to do it by trusting him."

Stephanie—on sexual addiction:

"Since I recognized I was a sex addict, I've sought healing and a closer relationship with God. Realizing I had crossed the line into addiction scared me. Sometimes I fantasize about guys when I am under a lot of stress. I've had to change my lifestyle a lot since I realized I do this. God's promises are coming true in my life as I am faithful to do my part. I *am* doing my part and that feels great."

Justin—on pornography:

"Those images stick with you. I mean, there were those nights at my dad's house I can't forget just because of those images, you know. It definitely messes with your mind. . . . Christ, he can heal all things. I do forgive myself for that, and I know God has forgiven me for that."

Jordan—on crossing boundaries and making out with girls:

"Jesus makes it very clear. He said if you even lust after a woman, you've already committed the act in your heart. And for me it's the issue of the heart, you know. So now I just want to live my life by the example Jesus set. So as far as my 'boundary' goes— yeah, no more. I definitely want to wait in every aspect of it." (Jordan references Matthew 5:27, 28, in his comment about Jesus' words.)

Nicole—on sexual compromise, two unplanned pregnancies, and one abortion:

"God loves me and sees me completely free and washed clean from my past. I pray that God will continue to heal me and mold me more like him. I pray that because of all the work and healing I have done, I will be able to enjoy sex like God created it to be."

Nicole *will* be able to enjoy sex like God created it to be, and so will any of us who take his plan for sex seriously. Talk to someone who has. They'll tell you—it's so worth it.

SEDUCED BY SEX : SAVED BY LOVE

> For some, a fresh start hasn't seemed possible. God can bring them back and set them on a path of healing and restoration. Don't assume they know that. Tell them.

FROM WEARINESS TO FREEDOM

The book of Proverbs reads, at times, like a letter from a father to a son, but its message of wisdom and warning could easily arrive in any of our mailboxes. Each of us can see it as a letter from a parent or from someone in our lives who loves us and hopes for the best for us. Or it could be a letter from God.

The fifth chapter of Proverbs has specific warnings about false intimacy. The opening verses describe the seductive invitation from those who might lure you into sexual traps—traps that seem as enticing as "dripping honey" but really are poisonous and painful. From the writer comes this advice: Don't even go to the door of that house. Don't put yourself anywhere near the situation (v. 8).

This "letter" also warns what happens when you dip into what seems to be the promise of pleasure. There is a guarantee of pain, emptiness, and exhaustion: "At the end of your life you will groan, when your flesh and body are spent. You will say, 'How I hated discipline! How my heart spurned correction! I would not obey my teachers or listen to my instructors. I have come to the brink of utter ruin'" (Proverbs 5:11-14).

Groaning and soul weariness don't necessarily have to come at the end of a person's life. They can come much sooner, as was the case with Suzy. But a wake-up call—that's a good thing. This type of lifestyle is one that could use a major interruption.

OK, fast forward to Jesus' time and you can take a look at a situation where someone experienced this kind of life interruption. In John 8 you read about Jesus teaching the religious guys who thought they had it all together. While Jesus is there, they bring in a woman who has been sleeping around, cheating on her husband. (Conveniently for them, they choose to not bring in the man who was part of the affair.) According to the Jewish law of that time, she was to be killed by stoning. Jesus gives any one of the guys there the opportunity to go ahead and do that—*if* he can claim he hasn't sinned. Of course, they all walk away. None of them can condemn her. Jesus turns to the woman and tells her he won't condemn her either, but then he adds, "Go now and leave your life of sin" (John 8:11).

So take all that together. The warning for any of us is urgent. We're to stay far away from situations that might cause us to be a part of false intimacy and compromise. If we go there, we will experience pain, deep regret, and weariness of soul. If we have already gone there, Jesus looks us in the eyes, and with unimaginable love and compassion, pleads, "Go now (not tomorrow) and leave (without any consideration of returning) your life of sin."

Do you see the great mercy in those words? The forgiveness? The love? The freedom? It's for you. God's letter written on your heart.

God, I see the small and big ways I've walked
not only up to the door of false intimacy but right
through it. Maybe in ways others can't see, but you

*do. You know my heart, my mind, my every action.
I come to you with my pain, my regret, my sadness,
and ask your forgiveness. Give me the strength
to start fresh. Help me remember your love and
mercy and never take them for granted.* AMEN.

> **And I will give them singleness of heart
> and put a new spirit within them.
> I will take away their stony, stubborn heart
> and give them a tender, responsive heart.**
>
> EZEKIEL 11:19 (NLT)

GOING DEEPER

■ Time for a heart check. What in your life right now is keeping you at a distance from God and from really going after the kind of life he has planned for you?

■ In what ways are you walking right up to or through the door of sexual compromise? How do you see that now in light of the warnings in Proverbs 5?

■ Do you struggle believing God can forgive you and give you a fresh beginning? How does Jesus' interaction with the woman in John 8 change that for you?

DEEPER STILL

Read Proverbs 5. Think of someone you know who really cares about you. Write a letter, something similar to Proverbs 5, that that person would write to *you*. Address the specific struggles you may be having. End the letter with a similar response as that of Jesus, when he told the woman in John 8 to go and sin no more.

SEDUCED BY SEX : SAVED BY LOVE

ten

I was weak, and I knew it, and I knew if I went back to my high school, I'd make the same decisions over and over again.

"I THINK YOU'RE READY TO GO BACK."

Mom stood in Suzy's bedroom doorway. Suzy had taken a break from school for a few days and was going to try it again today.

"I don't think I am." Her tightened stomach, the shaking she felt inside, screamed that she wasn't ready.

"Well, give it a try and we'll see."

She wished she could share Mom's optimism. But her mother just didn't understand how hard being at school was for her. The prayer with the women had helped, but the sense of hope and lightness she had felt after that time was now shadowed by an anxiety that rattled her confidence.

She walked toward the front door, dreading opening it and actually going to school. Then she stopped. Maybe there was a way to get through the day. Maybe even get out of it. She turned into the kitchen and stood in front of the cabinet where medicines and prescriptions were kept. She shifted a few bottles and packets until she found Mom's prescription for antidepressant. She poured a few into her hand, and then a few more, until fifteen of the tiny white pills lay in one palm. She stared at them. Enough to make her sick? Enough to get her sent home? Maybe enough to get her excused from school for the two and a half months that were left? She took down a glass

ten

from another cabinet, filled it with water, and took the pills. All fifteen of them.

> **The prayer with the women had helped, but the sense of hope and lightness she had felt after that time was now shadowed by an anxiety that rattled her confidence.**

In first period, she began to fill woozy; second period, sick to her stomach. She asked to be dismissed. In the restroom, she hung onto the sink, willing herself to stay upright. A staff person came in while she clung to the counter.

As the woman began to pass her, she eyed Suzy. "What's going on?"

Suzy felt no reason to lie. "I took some of my mom's antidepressant. I feel sick."

The woman's eyes narrowed. Her lips spread into a firm line. "You did *what?*"

Suzy closed her eyes and held on tighter to the sink.

"You need to go to the nurse. Come with me." She grabbed Suzy by the arm.

Suzy pulled her arm away. "I can walk." *Kind of.* All she knew was that she didn't want this lady jerking her to the nurse's office.

Suzy tried to focus on the IV tube that strung down to her arm from the bottle in the attendant's hand. Through the fuzziness of the drug, she struggled to think. She was getting

SEDUCED BY SEX : SAVED BY LOVE

out of school, but was this worth it? She didn't know yet. She didn't want to die. That thought flashed through her mind a couple of times that morning, but really all she wanted was for the pressure to end. Not her life. Had she gone too far? The dizziness made her nauseous.

Poor Mom. She had met her in the nurse's office at school and had looked so scared. Now she was following the ambulance in her car. Suzy felt sad. She wanted her parents to understand why she couldn't be at school but hadn't thought how hard this would be for them.

In the emergency room the staff gave Suzy liquid coal to absorb the drugs in her system. When they felt she was stabilized, they transferred her to the top floor of the hospital to be admitted to the psych ward. She was placed on a suicide watch. The rest of that day, and the next few, blurred together. Her parents, quiet and sad, visited and sat with her.

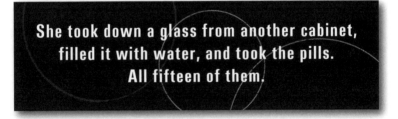

She took down a glass from another cabinet, filled it with water, and took the pills. All fifteen of them.

On one of those days, Sharon, Luanne, and Cetina came by. They surrounded her bed, smiles spread across their faces like they shared some secret. Mom and Dad were there too. Suzy looked around the room. She felt comfortable with all of them. She didn't have to pretend to be anyone except who she was. That felt good.

"Let's sing," Luanne offered, and the women started in as if it were their plan.

One song after another filled the room. Suzy felt tense and self-conscious about what others in the hospital must be thinking, but as she listened she began to feel the hope the women held for her. She closed her eyes, willing that hope to carry her into the days ahead.

> **She didn't have to pretend to be anyone except who she was. That felt good.**

Then they began another song, the words washing over Suzy: "*. . . Nothing is too difficult for thee, nothing is too difficult for thee . . .*"

Suzy wanted to feel the truth of that, but even more she wanted her parents to know God was great and mighty and nothing too difficult for him. She watched their faces. Dad looked less sad; Mom appeared more calm.

Luanne asked Suzy what she planned to do when she was released.

"I don't know yet." She looked toward Mom and Dad. No one really knew.

A couple of days later, Suzy was alone in her room. Her week's stay in the hospital would be over soon. An attendant came in and handed her the phone. Her father wanted to talk to her.

"Hi, Dad."

"Hi, honey. I wanted to tell you, I just had this . . . I don't know what to call it." He seemed to be wrestling with words. He went on. "I went to the grocery store, and when I was getting back into the car, well . . . I got this sentence in my head."

What is he talking about? Still, Dad sounded different, upbeat—especially considering his usual even nature. "What sentence, Dad?"

"*Suzy is going to be OK*—that's the sentence," her dad said. Relief tinged his voice. "I really believe it's true. You're going to be OK."

Suzy felt a rush of peace. "Do you think that's what God is saying?" She hoped God was still with her, even when she kept making these choices that turned into messes for everyone.

"It could be."

Maybe it was a new thought to him, but Suzy could tell her father was ready to give God the credit, and she definitely wanted to.

> **Suzy felt a rush of peace.**
> **"Do you think that's what God is saying?"**
> **She hoped God was still with her.**

She hung up and dropped her head back onto her pillow. Dad seemed so convinced, but she wondered about Luanne's earlier question about what was next for her. She still didn't know what to do about school. She'd have to trust that God knew, even if it confused everyone else. Would she really be OK?

ten

> God can do anything, you know—far more than you could ever imagine or guess or request in your wildest dreams! He does it not by pushing us around but by working within us, his Spirit deeply and gently within us.
>
> EPHESIANS 3:20 (THE MESSAGE)

A PROCESS

What went wrong? Five and a half hours of prayer. Shouldn't that have been more than enough to turn things around for someone? Suzy seemed so changed. So hopeful.

When Suzy overdosed and went to the hospital, Sharon saw it as a suicide attempt. It didn't make sense. In her mind, their prayers had battled the fiercest enemies of Suzy's soul and broken down walls. She said, "I felt very disappointed and had to call Luanne and Cetina and even other people at that point and ask, 'Why isn't this working?' This didn't fit with my theological world. There was supposed to have been victory and you're done and you go on. Little did I know that it's quite a process to set a person free."

It *is* a process, and their prayers were not empty ones. God's spirit was working in Suzy's heart at a deep level. Each person involved, including Suzy, would find their way to hold on to that as not just a possibility but as truth.

Karen's journal entry the day after Suzy went into the hospital read: "Lord, I don't have the wisdom to know what to do about Suzy, but that's OK. You do . . . Suzy's is not too tough a case for you. Give us all your wisdom for this situation. I believe the point of this particular lesson is for us to believe you are in charge. You are more than able to keep Suzy, or anyone."

A turning point for Suzy's family was when Sharon, Luanne, and Cetina visited and sang "Nothing Is Too Difficult for Thee"—an older song with an upbeat rhythm. The women sang it with a lot of energy and the belief that it was fully true for Suzy's situation. Sharon said, "Suzy's dad told me later he knew during that song that there was hope. Before that he was just ready to throw in the towel."

Suzy was encouraged by that visit too, and even more a few days later when her dad called and said he felt the confidence that she was going to be OK. She said, "God gave him peace as a daddy, as a father. It gives me a huge lump in my throat thinking about what my parents went through with me and for me."

Don, Suzy's dad, remembers how the entire situation made a huge impact in his and Connie's lives. "You know, up until that time, Connie and I had been going to church, but we weren't strong Christians. Or at least I wasn't a practicing Christian. So that's something that gave me more focus on my relationship with God." When asked how the events changed him, he said, "The difference was that I went to church to worship God, and from then on I started to focus on my responsibilities as a husband and a father instead of focusing on work and those kinds of things."

It was a scary and difficult situation for all of them, especially Suzy. But God had this one covered too. Nothing is too difficult for him.

> God hasn't left the scene when things take a bad turn. Be spiritually strong in what you believe about struggles and suffering long before someone calls on you for encouragement and prayer.

GOOD COMPANY

Discouragement. Depression. Struggles to fight temptations or longings. Hopelessness in getting out of a situation. Throwing off an unwanted reputation. These were the emotions and thoughts with which Suzy wrestled.

Choosing a new direction is hard enough. Sticking to it can feel over-the-top impossible. But God never intends for us to face these battles alone. We all need friends and people we can count on for support, people who will go the distance with us, who will encourage us and pray for us while we're taking a different path than we have in the past.

At first Suzy wasn't sure who she could turn to or if she was even ready to ask for help. But then it was time, and the right people were there. She said, "It's so neat because they'll come out of the woodwork. They really will. I don't know how all those amazing women came to care for me, but when God is working in your situation, all you have to do is open your eyes just a little bit, and look at who's interested in you. And you've got your support system."

Those who came through for Suzy were the people in her church community. Others, besides the women who prayed for her, spent time with her, encouraged her, kept her on track. And she had friends like Camee who she could count on. "They had an obvious heart for me," Suzy said.

It'll also be obvious when they don't. Justin grew up in the church and had friends he'd known for a long time. He'd gotten the message that sexual purity was a big deal. He said, "We all respected that, like, having sex was something sacred. 'We don't go near sex.' But it just broke down. Skipping church, leaving with girls, just doing stuff. And I still hadn't had sex, cause I was still, like—that was something sacred. And I thought, 'I'm just not going to do that.' But then, over time . . . First, it started [with] just kissing, then, OK, kissing a little more, hands sliding places, and pretty soon doing stuff at church. First Corinthians 15 [says] 'Bad company corrupts good habits.'"

What Justin needed was "good company." When he decided he really wanted that, he found it right in the same church.

Jordan did too. He struggled with pornography, among other stumbles. He said, "Man, through high school, [and] starting with probably junior high, pornography entered into the picture. And that is such a huge stumbling block for a lot of men and a lot of women." He realized he couldn't handle this one on his own. "Pretty much my only way to really cope with that and to try to get out of it was accountability, accountability, accountability. Like my youth pastor—I would talk to him and stay in communication with him."

Jordan also discovered support in good friends. "Some of the guys here have accountability partners, and we just talk to each other and call each other on the phone. We ask how our day's been going and pray with each other and just keep encouraging each other. That definitely helps."

Your "good company" possibilities? They might be adults you can trust who are solid in their values and faith; pastors who are available to mentor, disciple, and provide accountability support; or great friends who live out their faith in God and who want to keep growing.

Barbara Wilson, an abstinence educator in Sacramento, California, and author of *The Invisible Bond*, turns to James 4:7 and 2 Corinthians 10:3-5 to provide some direction. Regarding those verses, she said, "Success will come from relying on God for strength—submitting yourself to him every time you are tempted, resisting the enemy, and taking every thought captive." It's crucial, she added, to get healing from "your past sexual encounters and break the ungodly bonds you've created." She suggests "dating people and having friends who support your goals, people who hold you firmly accountable."

It takes a determination on your part to gravitate toward healthy situations and the people who will support you instead of the ones who will drag you down. If you're willing, the right people are there. Don't go it alone.

Set up a network with the youth you're leading so they can offer accountability for each other. Provide tools and instruction on how to do it well. Check up often on how it's working for the members of your group.

Before It Gets 'Too Difficult'

What ends up happening in sex starts way before the actual act. Except in the cases of abuse and rape, sex is a *choice*—not an accident.

Second Timothy 2:22 says, "Run from anything that stimulates youthful lusts" (*NLT*), and 1 Corinthians 6:18 has a similar warning: "Run from sexual sin! No other sin so clearly affects the body as this one does. For sexual immorality is a sin against your own body" (*NLT*).

Notice that both verses tell us to run. Why so strong? So we don't hang around and just see what will happen. Or casually walk away and look back from time to time. Nope. We're to run from sexual sin.

But if you're running, it's kind of nice to not only know what you're running from, but also what you're running toward. The second half of 2 Timothy 2:22 gives us that: "Instead, pursue righteous living, faithfulness, love, and peace. Enjoy the companionship of those who call on the Lord with pure hearts" (*NLT*).

Pursue, chase after, and practice those things that will keep you from lust and sexual compromise. Spend time with and enjoy the friendship and encouragement of those "who call on the Lord with pure hearts."

That brings us back to those friends, teachers, and mentors that we can gather around us for support and accountability. Every one of us needs that when—and even before—things get difficult.

God, some of the people I hang out with bring me down, and I'm not strong enough to keep from falling into the kind of talking they do, the choices they make. Help me to know ahead of time when I'm walking into a bad situation and need to get out of there. Show me where I need to spend more time with friends who will help me pursue righteous living. Help me find mentors and accountability partners who will take me closer to you so I can honor you in every area of my life and live more purely, especially when it comes to my relationships. AMEN.

He who walks with the wise grows wise, but a companion of fools suffers harm.

PROVERBS 13:20

GOING DEEPER

At school, at church—in any place—what kinds of people and situations do you find yourself gravitating toward? What can you do to make sure you're staying spiritually strong wherever you are?

■ Do your friends support your goals or bring you down? How can you set up a workable accountability situation either with them or with someone who cares about your progress?

■ What's going on in your life that is becoming too difficult for you? Who are the people around you who you can go to for encouragement and support?

DEEPER STILL

Memorize 2 Timothy 2:22. When you've got it down pretty well, go for a run. As you're running, think about the verse and what you personally want to run from and run toward. Pray and ask God to help you with those decisions.

eleven

I didn't want to meet God in quiet moments. I was afraid.
I was kind of living on other people's prayers.

"SUZY, THE CALL IS FOR YOU. IT'S LUANNE."

Suzy pushed herself up from the couch in the den and took the cordless from her mom. "Thanks." She slid into one of the dining room chairs.

"Hi."

"How are you doing?" Luanne's voice was cheerful, but Suzy knew her question went much deeper than just a greeting.

> She thought of Luanne's question in
> the hospital—what would she do when
> she got home?

"OK. Still tired a lot."

"Doing much since you've been home?"

"Not really. Just resting. Hanging around home."

"What's next for you?"

She thought of Luanne's question in the hospital—what would she do when she got home? A lot of people, especially Sharon, didn't feel Edward's High School was a good place for her right now. She agreed. Just thinking about facing it again made her queasy.

"I don't want to go back to school."

"It doesn't seem like a good environment for you right now."

Suzy ran her finger along the ridged edge of the dining room table. "I know." A thought had been playing in her mind even while she was in the hospital. "I . . . I'd like to come stay with you."

The line was silent. Suzy closed her eyes and held her breath. *Should I have said that?*

Finally, Luanne answered. "I had prayed for that, but I wanted it to be your decision. You saying it confirms for me that God might want it too." The line was quiet again before she said, "Let's see how we can make it happen."

Suzy exhaled and smiled. "OK."

Over the next few minutes, Luanne arranged things with Mom and Dad. Suzy wouldn't be required to quit smoking yet—she had other areas to focus on. She would share a room with Mike and Luanne's daughter. During her stay she could continue her education through homeschool lessons, and she'd have the opportunity to attend a Bible study with Luanne. Suzy's parents agreed to give it a try.

> **"I had prayed for that, but I wanted it to be your decision. You saying it confirms for me that God might want it too."**

Suzy felt excited and hopeful. Maybe God really was working to make things OK.

 SEDUCED BY SEX : SAVED BY LOVE

At Luanne's, Suzy sat down on the mustard-colored couch in the living room, folding one of her legs under her. She leaned an elbow on the armrest and began flipping through the pages of a workbook she'd received as part of a Bible study she attended with Luanne. She didn't mind this kind of homework.

She read the words of the workbook as it explained how God wanted to pursue a real, and personal, relationship with her. She stopped.

God is pursuing me? She never thought of him that way. Her mind started working. *Why would he pursue me? Could I be lovely to him, even lovable?*

> **She was ready to stop running. She was done with lies and being someone she didn't like. She wanted to find out who the real Suzy was.**

She read down the page, filling in her answers to the questions, writing her thoughts. She stopped and settled her pen on the page as the message of the study began to sink in. Was it saying she could have a *relationship* with God?

Sitting there, she began to feel his love, to know that he wasn't someone far away. Tears warmed her cheeks as she realized for the first time that she didn't need to be afraid of his presence in the room with her. He could be near, and she wanted him near. Even the forgiveness she had asked for a few weeks before began to take on new meaning. He had given her freedom from her past choices. Now she felt she could really know him.

She closed her eyes and let out a breath. She was ready to stop running. She was done with lies and being someone she didn't like. She wanted to find out who the real Suzy was.

Karen handed Suzy a potted marigold. Suzy sat it on the ground and dug her trowel in the dirt. She was still staying at Luanne's, but Karen picked her up occasionally just to hang out. Today she was helping plant flowers in the terraced beds on the slope in front of Karen's home.

"Sharon told my parents about a ministry in California that maybe I can go to." She scooped out a hole for the plant. "You live there, and they have a high school."

"I heard about that. That's great." Karen brushed dirt from her arms and smiled.

"My parents called and asked some questions. I'm going to call and see if they'll send me an application." She pushed the clump of marigolds into a hole. "Sharon said she'd help me with the application." She stood. "Right now there's a waiting list."

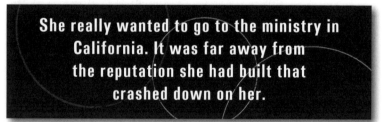

She really wanted to go to the ministry in California. It was far away from the reputation she had built that crashed down on her.

"We'll just have to pray that you'll get to the top of the list if that's where God wants you to be." Karen picked up the hose and watered some flowers. "Well, that does it here. You want to go for a walk?"

Suzy nodded. She planned to move back to her parents' place soon, but in the meantime she enjoyed spending time with Karen and Sharon when she could. She really wanted to go to the ministry in California. It was far away from the friends she had gotten into trouble with, far away from the reputation she had built that crashed down on her. Along with the new start God had given her, she wanted a new start away from this town.

She hoped the application would come in the mail soon. Then Sharon could help her with it. Excitement churned in her mind and stomach. Maybe it was the right place for her.

"So how's that? It's five pages." Sharon scooted her chair away from the desk, where she had been working at the computer.

I am struggling to keep my perspective while at home. I am not in school and feel very isolated and lonely. I continue to struggle with depression and other emotions.

Suzy leaned toward the monitor to look again at her autobiography, which Sharon had typed for her application. "Looks great," she said after reading through it again.

Sharon smiled, pulled herself back toward the desk, and clicked the mouse. "Let's print it off so you can get it sent."

As the printer hummed Suzy thought about the last few weeks. She'd stayed at Luanne's a little more than a month and then moved back home. School was almost out, but everyone agreed that she shouldn't go back. If she got accepted at the ministry in California, she'd continue her schoolwork there. If not—well, she didn't want to think about that. She *had* to get accepted. Her parents said she needed something like a greenhouse, where she could be safe and grow. She felt that too.

The pages came off the printer and Suzy picked them up. She read it through one final time, tears threatening at different parts, but really streaking down her cheeks as she finished the last few paragraphs . . .

> . . . *I moved back home on April 21ˢᵗ. I am struggling to keep my perspective while at home. I am not in school and feel very isolated and lonely. I continue to struggle with depression and other emotions. I am starting to meet with two women on the prayer team who will be helping me keep on track.*
>
> *I believe I have a long way to go in learning how to keep my life on a steady course. I have so much to learn and I am willing. I love the Lord so much for what he has done for me. He has been my refuge, my deliverer, and my strength. Without him I wouldn't be here today. I was hurting, and he held me.*
>
> *Please prayerfully consider my application.*
> *Thank you for your time.*

Please. If only those who would read it could sense the urgency she felt at that moment. She folded the pages with the rest of the application. *God, let there be an opening for me there.*

> **You came near when I called you,**
> **and you said, "Do not fear."**
>
> LAMENTATIONS 3:57

NO MORE RUNNING

Out of breath—and nowhere else to go. And all along God was there, saying to Suzy, "I'm here. Stop running. I love you."

"I was probably running from God pretty hard until that day at Luanne's," she recalled later. "But I was weary of running from him, running from the truth."

Up to that point, Suzy knew she was created by God, and she had some idea of his grace—a grace she felt she had thrown away. But a *relationship* with him? That was different. In the past, relationships meant something difficult, expectations she couldn't meet. Sitting in Luanne's living room, working through her Bible study, it began to make sense: God wasn't pushing a bunch of impossible demands on her. He was pursuing her. He was after her heart.

"That was the first time I ever thought about that," she said. "He loves me? He *likes* me? He still wants me after all I've done and gone through? How could he? After that, I let him pursue me. I knew I wanted in and wanted healing."

Though staying at Luanne's couldn't be a long-term solution, for a time it provided rest for Suzy, especially from the pressures of the school crowd she had once wanted to be a part of. While there, she learned who she was as God's child and who he was as her pursuer. Luanne, Sharon, Karen, and others continued to teach and encourage that relationship. "The women were direct with me—good at getting right to the truth and telling me God's Word. I was very open to it. I was beginning to live on God's promises. I wouldn't have been able to do that without those people. There were so many miracles."

One of the miracles, when she saw the God who pursues at work in her life, was in her relationship with her dad. She said, "I remember being in church with my dad, and I was holding his hand. The sermon was so right on, and there was an inside understanding between my dad and I that God was working. We were both teary-eyed."

She had stopped running. Her desire now was to give God her heart.

> **Don't assume others know how to have a solid relationship with God. Keep in mind how crucial that relationship is in decisions to not compromise or to move away from compromise. Provide discipleship.**

DEEP DOWN RESPECT

Suzy was beginning to grasp God's pursuing love for her, beginning to understand who she wanted to be. And something was happening inside that she didn't plan on—she was gradually gaining self-confidence and self-respect. If God loved her and cared enough to pursue her, maybe she could respect herself. She didn't need empty relationships and sex to do that.

Stephanie found that to be true too. She said, "I became a new [person] in Christ. At first I was very uncomfortable and shaky. Over time, I've regained my self-confidence and am happy with the new 'me' God is creating." For Stephanie, that involved a choice to deal head-on with sexual addictions. She said, "This has taken complete surrender and obedience on my part. That is the only way I can be restored to what God would have for me."

A restoration like that goes deep into your heart. God loves you more than you can imagine. He wants a relationship with you and longs to heal your wounds and restore you to all you were meant to be. Getting that truth inside will help you value and respect yourself more.

Ryan now realizes how important that is. He said, "I know that God loves me so much that he was tortured and died for me so I can be free." Before Ryan discovered that truth, he made a lot of decisions, including those about sex, based on the approval of friends. Now he seeks to please God and says confidently, "I know who I am in the Lord."

Christine, who grew up with an abusive dad and later felt she was supposed do whatever guys asked her to, also gained self-respect when she saw herself the way God sees her. She said, "I am precious to him. I am his child. He loves me and doesn't want anything but goodness for me. When I see myself through his eyes and allow him to love me this way, I have a better picture of the way I should be treated."

Christine has that right. You deserve to be treated as the treasured child of God that you are. When you really get that, you won't fall for the lines that draw you into sexual compromise.

Ever hear some of these?

"Why not? We love each other."

"Don't you love me? Prove it."

"I want to share myself with you. Don't you want that?"

"What's the big deal? Everybody is doing it."

"Just this once. Nothing will happen."

"You're still a virgin? You've got to be the only one."

"Why not? Don't you find me attractive?"

"But this will bring us a lot closer."

You might hear these lines when faced with propositions of intercourse, oral sex, petting, or any form of sexual intimacy. They're manipulative. People who say stuff like that don't *really* care about you.

But God does, and he's pursuing you because you are valuable to him. That's solid ground for your self-respect. When someone gives you one of those lines, just say, "I'm worth far more than that. I'm waiting for the real deal."

Pay attention to friends you know who are struggling to scrape up some self-respect. They could be in danger of doing anything to get it. Help them discover what they're good at and invite them to use those strengths in a church or community project.

A Love That Frees

Suzy was getting it—God loved her, really loved her. It is an amazing love, an unconditional love given with unconditional grace. Though she knew she could no longer take it for granted, she finally realized she didn't have to do one thing to earn it. She couldn't.

Neither can we.

Arms stretched across the splintering wood of a cross, Jesus hung. Some looked at him and spit at him. "We don't need you," they sneered. Others wept, believing many people had made a huge mistake—surely he didn't belong there. He was traded for a common criminal and now hung between two others.

But he was completely innocent, completely pure. And he was meant to be there. God planned it. His pursuing love for us put him there.

What led to his decision began in a garden when the first two humans, Adam and Eve, turned their hearts from God, their creator. Though they were surrounded by perfect beauty and existence, they chose to believe a deceiver. He lied and told them that God was keeping the best from them, that they could have so much more. He seduced them into exchanging intimacy with God for a false promise of power and immortality.

Sound familiar? The longing exists in each of us. In our own ways, we've sneered at God and told him we don't need him, or believe him, or want him. That we have things to do without him. Our souls are created to be in harmony with him, yet we toss aside that intimacy for a false relationship. Into the arms of seduction we fall, thinking that our deepest needs—acceptance, love, desire for the right kinds of things—can be met elsewhere. And we come up empty. All of us.

"We all, like sheep, have gone astray, each of us has turned to his own way . . ."

But in the midst of all this, God pursues. And so he sent his Son, Jesus . . . and brought him to the cross. God knew the only possible way to bring us back into a relationship with him was through an ultimate sacrifice of love—the death of his only Son for our wrongs.

". . . and the Lord has laid on him the iniquity of us all" (Isaiah 53:6).

He did that . . . for you. For all of us.

Though seduced and fallen, we are saved by his great love—if we choose to respond to his prodding in our hearts.

Do you hear it? Feel it? God is pursuing you.

God, no one is exempt. I have in my own ways fallen for the lies that tell me you aren't enough. But you don't give up on me. You are in pursuit. You designed me to be in relationship with you. Forgive me for going my own way and making choices that are destructive to my body, my emotions, and especially my spirit. Though I come to you, I know the lies and seduction that pull me away from you won't stop. Help me see them for what they are and give me the strength to resist them. Help me live fully with you and for you. AMEN.

> He offered himself as a sacrifice to free us from a dark,
> rebellious life into this good, pure life, making us
> a people he can be proud of, energetic in goodness.
>
> TITUS 2:14 (THE MESSAGE)

GOING DEEPER

■ Think of yourself as one of those standing at the foot of the cross the day Jesus died. What would you say to him? What do your choices and actions say?

■ God pursued Suzy; he pursues a relationship with you. How does knowing that help you see your relationship with him differently? How does it help you value and respect yourself more?

■ When we say yes to false intimacy, we aren't respecting or valuing ourselves as God sees us. Have you found yourself in a situation like that? Think about how it made you feel and how you will respond in the future. Find a trustworthy friend and discuss these things.

DEEPER STILL

Consider this: "God loves me and is pursuing a relationship with me. In honoring him and who he created me to be, I can respect myself." Each day, for one week, keep track of the ways you felt that message was challenged. Journal how you responded and how you grew stronger.

SEDUCED BY SEX : SAVED BY LOVE

twelve

My parents shared that they were proud of me.
I cried and cried and cried because it felt so good to hear.

SUZY WIPED A SHELF and rearranged the cans and jars in the large walk-in panty. It was one of her chores for that week, one she often did since arriving at the residential ministry known by almost everyone as "The Ranch." Her application had been accepted and she arrived just after her birthday in July.

She grabbed the coffee tin of soapy water and stepped out of the pantry into the kitchen. As she sat the can down, she re-clipped the stray hairs that had fallen forward across her face. Her hair, now shoulder length, had grown out from the shorter style she had when she came here nine months earlier. She purposely had it cut in her desire to strip away anything she had relied on to feel accepted.

She glanced up at the clock by the kitchen sink. It was time to head to Gene's office for counseling. She pushed through the kitchen door. As she walked down the cement stairs toward the downstairs office, she heard the door creak and pound as it settled closed.

Gene's door, the first one at the bottom of the steps, was open slightly. She knocked softly and heard his "come on in." The office was small and L-shaped. Suzy made her way over to the couch at the back of the office. As usual, the smell of fresh, locally ground coffee filled the room. It was the signature aroma of this office and one most people associated with Gene.

He stood from his desk just inside the door, his large frame consuming the tiny room. With a quiet, contrasting voice he asked Suzy if she wanted a cup of coffee. She nodded and accepted a cup, curling the warm drink into both hands as she pulled her legs up and crossed them.

Gene sat in a chair across from her and ran his hand through his beard. They chatted about the day and what they would do for that session. Lately, at least once or twice a week, Gene arranged family meetings by calling her parents and using the speakerphone. It seemed to Suzy that each session brought new revelations about herself and her family. The progress felt exciting, though at times it also hit really hard. She never knew what to expect in each meeting.

"Are you ready to do this?"

> It seemed to Suzy that each session brought new revelations about herself and her family. The progress felt exciting, though at times it also hit really hard.

Suzy hesitated, then nodded. They both rose, and she settled into his desk chair while he dialed the phone and clicked on the speaker function. Both Gene and Suzy sipped coffee as the meeting got started. Everyone greeted each other, and then Gene gave a summary of what they'd recently covered and asked if anyone had any thoughts.

Suzy listened to the tone in her parents' voices, their words. They wondered how she was doing. They missed her.

Then Mom said, "Suzy, we want you to know we love you and we're proud of you." Dad voiced his agreement.

> **Gene put his hand on her shoulder and spoke to her parents. "Let me describe to you what I'm seeing here. Maybe you can hear her crying."**

At that moment, the conversation stopped for Suzy. Parents nearly anywhere, at nearly any time, can utter those words to their children, but for her, they were like water to a parched throat in the desert. Tears began to come, then sobs.

Gene put his hand on her shoulder and spoke to her parents. "Let me describe to you what I'm seeing here. Maybe you can hear her crying. She looks shaken by this." Then he turned to her. "Do you know what you're responding to?" he asked Suzy. "Do you want to tell them about that?"

She closed her eyes and wrapped her arms across herself. "It's hard to believe it," she forced out, through some hesitations. Tears were still coming. "It's good to hear." She didn't realize how much she needed to hear it, but God did. She could feel him directing this time. Though she didn't know what each phone conversation would bring, didn't have expectations of anything in particular, he was using these times to heal her family.

She realized the year before had been hard for all of them. Nothing she did would make anyone proud. And though she had been doing well at the Ranch, it felt like the words from her parents came unattached to anything she had done, without any expectations of what she would do in the days ahead. She now

twelve

felt it deep inside—their love for her, their pride, was simply because she was their daughter.

That thought carried her over the next few weeks.

On another day, Suzy was wiping the extra water from two deep kitchen sinks and turned to see if the others on her team had finished their part of dinner cleanup. They were done. Good. She'd find the intern in charge for the evening and get permission to go outside. Hanging around the dining room or living room was too hectic with everyone around. She wanted time to think.

She was given the OK and stepped outside, walked partway down the cement steps, and sat down. So much had happened in the last few weeks. She felt tired, but it was a good kind of tired. She had worked hard in school that day and finished all her chores in the work program. And all that without clashes with the other girls, which sometimes happened.

> **Her thoughts flashed back to a childhood moment. While she sat on the floor, knees pulled up, crying, she decided to write a poem.**

She looked out over the pond just a few feet away from the steps. A pair of wild ducks swam by the edges. Bullfrogs billowed and birds sang in the cattails. It was amazingly peaceful. She breathed a sigh.

She thought of the recent weeks. The call with Mom and Dad still played in her mind. *We love you. We're proud of you.*

Her thoughts flashed back to a childhood moment. Mom and Dad were mad about something she'd done and she'd gone to her room. While she sat on the floor, knees pulled up, crying, she decided to write a poem. She had called it "Jesus Loves Me Just Because I'm Me." The words were gone now, but she remembered the feeling of Jesus being there with her—almost as if he were tenderly stroking her hair. She could make all the mistakes in the world; he'd love her no matter what. Unconditionally.

> **At that moment Suzy couldn't guess the challenges and compromises ahead that would again push her to question her basis for acceptance. She had much more to learn about herself and about God.**

Sounds drifting from the open living room windows above her drew her back to the present. She could hear laughter, snatches of conversations. Several played guitars. She usually gravitated toward the activity, but it felt good to step away for a change.

She smiled as she identified the different voices and imagined what each person was doing. Their acceptance of her amazed her every day. Her attitude sometimes got her into trouble—like disagreements with other girls, like the time she got mad and punched a hole in her dorm wall. None of that changed the way they cared about her.

twelve

Unconditional love—just as Jesus had shown her as a little child—that's what she was experiencing here. She felt the contrast to what had driven her before—acceptance at any cost. And it had cost a lot.

Suzy heard the back door creak and slam closed and then footsteps walking toward her. She glanced up to see Jen, a college grad who was one of the interns. Her flip-flops slapped against the steps as she made her way to Suzy's step and sat down beside her.

"What's up, Suzy? You OK?" Her mood seemed light, but her question expressed concern.

Suzy smiled. It was so like the leaders at this place to check on people at different times to make sure they were OK. "Nothing. Things are good. I just wanted to sit out here and think for a while."

Jen didn't push for more. She just slipped her arm across Suzy's shoulders and hugged her.

At that moment Suzy couldn't guess the challenges and compromises ahead that would again push her to question her basis for acceptance. To really get it down into her heart, she had much more to learn about herself and about God.

> But because of his great love for us, God, who is rich in mercy, made us alive with Christ even when we were dead in transgressions—it is by grace you have been saved.
>
> EPHESIANS 2:4, 5

Sometimes we have to get far away from whatever is messing with our lives. Suzy stepped into a ministry environment two states away, badly needing safety from the strong peer influence she had felt. This new place would be her home for the next year, maybe two. "Tired, exhausted, used, and broken" is how she described herself when she arrived. She was ready for a change.

She came to a place that became her home away from home, with people that became like family. It was made up of ministry staff, teachers, interns, and teens and young adults like her who had faced pain or trouble and wanted to learn to live differently. Would these people—strangers to her—accept her as she was? She remembered, "I was so afraid and full of shame, but I [let out] the real Suzy." She was surprised to find that even as she told them some of her story they didn't judge her. "All I got was open arms. No wincing at the things I shared, just love. For the first time, I felt acceptable."

She quickly responded to that kind of acceptance. "I was becoming beautiful. The light inside was coming out. By the time I made my first visit back to my hometown, I was walking across the street, meeting people's eyes, giving smiles away because I wanted everyone to know the free grace I'd received. I was making eye contact with strangers because I knew that in Christ I was worthy to do so."

For her, the family life at the Ranch gave her a sense of how relationships could work differently than she'd known. "Before, my faith in other people and in myself was built on conditional love, so the Ranch gave me a working model of the way God designed the family—a working model of unconditional love."

Suzy stayed at the Ranch almost two years before returning home. During that time she had seventeen counseling sessions—out of more than one hundred, in all—that included phone talks with her parents and her counselor. Most of the specific details of those sessions are forgotten, but the one phone call when her parents expressed their pride in her made a lasting impression. She hadn't realized how much she needed to hear them say those words. At the same time, she doesn't blame them for not saying them more often. "It's not that my parents didn't say that before, but it was the first time I was able to hear that, with no strings attached, I was lovable," she said.

A lot of growth happened for Suzy at the Ranch, but the key for her was that knowledge—she was lovable. Within a good environment, surrounded by people who did their best to model Christ's love, she was learning she could be herself and develop values that supported a Suzy she liked.

> Be part of creating a community—in your home or church—where people can be themselves, make mistakes, and keep growing and living out their Christian faith. Make it a community that models how to have healthy guy-girl friendships.

GOOD CONNECTIONS

Suzy's desire to feel loved and accepted had driven her into the arms of false intimacy, and she discovered those experiences were just that—false, unsatisfying, and empty. Trying to belong by being someone she wasn't, sneaking out, hanging out with different guys, and having sex hadn't made her feel any more loved or accepted. What did? Connecting with people who knew all about her and didn't expect anything but the real Suzy. No strings attached, as she put it.

Through her story, you've already seen some of those people—friends her age and women who were mentors to her. Some prayed with her. Others invited her into their home, spent time with her by doing simple things like planting flowers, taking walks, talking. Some just sat with her and let her be . . . Suzy. More, like those at the Ranch, challenged her to grow in some hard ways, to be disciplined and strive to do her best in her school and work, to develop skills and interests, and to know Jesus more deeply.

Every one of those people modeled love to her. The message she'd heard as a child—*Jesus loves me just because I'm me*—came through loud and clear. She was in an environment where she could gain a sense of who she was at the core. As they showed her love and acceptance as Jesus would, she began to do the same. That's the beauty of having positive models in your life.

But some models are destructive.

Kelly's family grew up going to church. Her mother was actively involved and her father was a workaholic and an alcoholic, but the family *looked* together. Kelly watched the adults in her life pretend to be perfect. Their model: impossible standards, conditional love.

Ryan's family did not have a Christian foundation. He felt his parents' love, but also was confused in watching how they expressed love to each other. Affection seemed superficial. Fights and unfaithfulness eventually ended the marriage.

Abuse is also a destructive model, as it was for Christine, who was verbally and physically abused; Nicole, who was sexually abused; Justin, who grew up around pornography in his father's house; and Reese, who was placed in a foster home in a neighborhood where he was beat up and raped.

Models etch impressions in our lives—for good or bad. But we can always move toward better ones. Getting grounded, avoiding sexual situations, staying on track, healing hurts—all of these are best accomplished in the context of real and solid relationships.

The couple mentioned in an earlier chapter, Amanda and Kevin, found two couples they look to. Amanda watched her best friend meet someone and fall in love. Amanda said, "Instead of doing like us, where we pursued those moments to be alone so we could push ourselves together, when they got to a place where they could slip (sexually), they had self-restraint, got out of the situation, and went to be around people they knew." This couple, young when they met, waited six years to marry. "They did it right," Amanda said. "They have an amazing marriage."

Amanda and Kevin also look to an older couple as their role models and mentors. They observe their marriage, their ministry, and their character and see them, as Kevin puts it, as "very awesome people."

SEDUCED BY SEX : SAVED BY LOVE

Sometimes an awesome example is right in front of you. Jason is a California youth pastor for a large group ranging from junior high to college. The teens and young adults in the ministry look up to him. He disciples, mentors, and counsels his group, loving them through and out of their messes. He teaches them how to study the Bible, really think through their values and faith in Jesus, and then shows them how to live that faith out with their friends and in their community—including through an intense street ministry. While he was engaged to be married, those in his group watched how he chose to honor his wife-to-be by waiting for any form of intimate touching until after they were married. And the group respects all of that in Jason. You can see it in their eyes and in their words. They look up to him because they see him living, the best he can, like Jesus.

> Being seen as a model or a mentor isn't worth much unless it's rooted in a relationship with Jesus Christ that translates to solid values. What are people admiring in you? Looking up to? Can they say it's because you're living like Jesus?

Living Close

Living like Jesus—it can be a tall order for someone you're looking to for a role model. But it's a tall order for each of us. God calls us to watch and imitate those whose lives reflect Jesus, then work toward being a similar example to those around us. When we grab hold of that, we tend to take living out our faith and values more seriously.

twelve

How to begin? The only way is by living close to Jesus. John 15:4, 5 says, "Remain in me, and I will remain in you. No branch can bear fruit by itself; it must remain in the vine. Neither can you bear fruit unless you remain in me. I am the vine; you are the branches. If a man remains in me and I in him, he will bear much fruit; apart from me you can do nothing."

Remain. Stay connected. Grow familiar with what it means to take Jesus into every area of your life. Study his life and walk. Pray, serve, and love like he did. The result will be the kind of productive life that only comes by living close to Jesus—the kind of life that is an example for others, especially living a life of no compromise, sexually or otherwise.

We can take seriously the same warning Jesus gave his followers: "One day Jesus said to his disciples, 'There will always be temptations to sin, but what sorrow awaits the person who does the tempting! It would be better to be thrown into the sea with a millstone hung around your neck than to cause one of these little ones to fall into sin'" (Luke 17:1-2, *NLT*).

People are watching you, getting their cues from you on what they should do. Make your example count.

God, it's amazing the people who have had an impact on my life—for good and for bad. Help me to heal from those situations that have caused deep wounds, and help me cling to the life-examples that more closely reflect your ways. Help me to get the model of your Son, Jesus, down deep in my life so I'm able to not only live like he did, but also pass on a good example to others. AMEN.

> And don't let anyone put you down because you're young.
> Teach believers with your life:
> by word, by demeanor, by love, by faith, by integrity.
> 1 TIMOTHY 4:12 (THE MESSAGE)

GOING DEEPER

■ Some of our models for relationships have been destructive. Their influences have made our lives hard. What ways do you need to trust God to help shake those influences?

■ Look at the most revealing characteristics of your life that show how you handle relationships. Whose life have you most watched and followed as a model? Do you see others who could encourage you to know Jesus more deeply?

■ Whether you've chosen to or not, you're an example to others around you. What specific steps can you take to live more like Jesus and model his life more openly and powerfully?

DEEPER STILL

Add a section to your journal as you read more deeply in the New Testament. Write down what you learn from Jesus' life: how he interacted with people, responded to situations, what he said. Write your specific thoughts on ways you can follow his example.

thirteen

*I thought I was in love. I wanted it to work, but deep inside
I knew it wasn't right because of the choices I made
to be so intimate before marriage.*

Suzy pushed through the heavy wooden door into the sports bar, where she was to meet Sasha, a friend from her college, and Sasha's boyfriend. They wanted to introduce her to someone.

She stopped just inside the door and took a deep breath. It had been awhile since she even thought of dating anyone. She'd only been home from the Ranch for a few months. In that time, she'd been busy—starting college classes, finding a job working at a clothing store, and then moving into a condo with a friend. Now Sasha wanted to set up a date for Suzy with her boyfriend's buddy, Brent.

She hoped she looked OK. Sasha spotted her and waved her over.

As she slipped into the booth she smiled. "Hi, I'm Suzy."

He nodded his head and grinned. "Brent. Good to meet you."

The waitress stopped by and Suzy ordered an iced tea. She turned her attention back to the conversation. Brent seemed easygoing, comfortable. He was a cowboy. Polite. Nice smile. Brown eyes, brown hair. She wanted to know more.

They chatted and snacked on fried mozzarella sticks, then decided to go to Suzy's condo to watch a movie. She felt relaxed and comfortable with Brent. He seemed different from other guys she'd known—he didn't put any moves on her.

The next day she heard from Sasha that Brent said he couldn't stop thinking of her. That was nice to hear. She'd give him a call.

A few nights later the two of them were at his place watching TV, relaxing after an afternoon of hiking. They were sitting on the floor with their backs to the couch.

She realized he was staring at her and smiling. "Yes?"

He cocked his head sideways. "Would it be OK if I kissed you?"

Wow, he was actually asking. That was new. "Yes," she answered.

> **She felt relaxed and comfortable with Brent. He seemed different from other guys she'd known—he didn't put any moves on her.**

He bent his head toward her with a light touch of his lips on hers. She leaned into the kiss, then let it linger and grow. He pulled her into a closer embrace, and she ran her hand behind his neck, pressing her tongue into his mouth. Feelings stirred that she had felt before.

He pulled away, but still held her. "Whoa—I just meant a little kiss."

Suzy's face reddened. "I'm sorry. I thought—"

"Oh, no, I liked it." He smiled.

Suzy stood. "I better go."

"OK."

Feelings stirred that she had felt before. He pulled away, but still held her.

They both stood and Suzy got her things. Brent walked her to the door. Suzy got into her car, still flushed. Wasn't that what he expected her to do? She sighed. She really liked him. Had she blown it already? He probably wouldn't want to see her again.

But he did. Over the next few weeks they spent a lot of time together. At her place. More often at his. The more time they spent alone with each other, the more time they spent on the couch engaged in intense physical contact.

Suzy stood up from the couch, adjusting her clothes. She headed down Brent's hallway. He came out of the bathroom and met her in the hall. She put her arms around his neck.

"Suzy."

"What?"

"I don't . . ." He seemed to wrestle with the right words to say.

"Brent?"

"It's just that I want to be sure when I have sex, it's with the one I'm going to marry."

thirteen

"OK." Suzy pulled away. "I understand." Yes, she understood—he was rejecting her. What else could it be? Guys didn't turn down sex.

Back at her place, she turned on some of her favorite Christian music, and let the tears come. She liked Brent. Maybe they *would* get married someday. Her thoughts turned into a confused jumble, one moment hurt that Brent rejected her offer, and the next angry at herself.

She was doing the double life thing again.

> **They'd crossed lines. How could they go back? With the guilt draping her, she slid down the wall of her condo and sobbed.**

She was active in leadership in the church, working with the junior high students, and then living out a different standard with Brent—one she knew compromised values she thought she had grasped more solidly. It all felt natural—*too* natural. She had taken that first step with Brent, inviting him with the first kiss. Then she helped set the tone for their times together, allowing each successive kiss to lead to much more—everything short of intercourse.

They'd crossed lines. How could they go back? With the guilt draping her, she slid down the wall of her condo and sobbed.

Their relationship continued on the same course. One day she got a call from Brent. He was upset. His dog, a childhood

 SEDUCED BY SEX : SAVED BY LOVE

pet and hunting companion, was dying.

"I'll come right now. Which vet?"

Suzy hung up and drove to meet him. She could tell he was broken up over it. She pulled her car into the clinic parking lot; Brent was already standing outside. Suzy slid out of the car and held him. "I'm so sorry, Brent."

He shook his head. He seemed to have no words.

She rubbed his arm. "You want to come over?"

"Sure." His voice was flat.

They drove separately to Suzy's parents' house; she had moved back in recent weeks. She unlocked the door and they went in.

"I'll make you something to eat." Suzy watched him while she gathered what she needed to make some sandwiches. He was so sad. How could she help?

They ate in silence. When they finished, Suzy stood and went to him, wrapping him in her arms. She kissed his head, his cheek, his lips, and he responded. She kissed him more and they moved into the den, their emotions carrying them into more. She now knew how she'd comfort him. She stood and looked at him. He stood too.

> **Suzy huddled by the altar in tears, her sadness deep. How could she walk into this lifestyle again?**

"Are you sure?"

He nodded.

Together they walked to her back bedroom.

At church, Suzy huddled by the altar in tears, her sadness deep. How could she walk into this lifestyle again? Her friend and mentor, Karen, came over and knelt by her. Suzy couldn't tell her what tore at her heart.

She cared about Brent but their relationship had headed the wrong way. She blamed herself. And though Brent had started coming to church, she didn't know what it meant to him. One time early in their relationship he had said that if his being a Christian mattered to her, they might as well stop right there. But they didn't.

In her sorrow, she once again felt God calling her back. She didn't feel she deserved it, but she longed for it. She needed to get away to think, to figure out how to start fresh again.

> Let us then approach the throne of grace with confidence,
> so that we may receive mercy
> and find grace to help us in our time of need.
>
> HEBREWS 4:16

CAUGHT UP AGAIN

A confident Suzy had left the safety of the Ranch not realizing that some battles were not yet conquered in her life. Sex had a hold on her in a way she didn't realize.

"I thought I was further along than I was," she said. In trying to figure out why later, she could only say, "Remnants of old expectations." Emotions and passions were stirred, echoes of "You started it, finish it." She said of her relationship with Brent, "Things got intense pretty fast. Once I was in it, I was caught in it again."

And the thing was, Suzy did feel Brent loved her for who she was. She didn't need sex for acceptance this time. Sex felt right because she thought they cared about each other, maybe even loved each other. And yet it felt all wrong too. Wrestling with her guilt, wrestling with God, she couldn't sleep at night. "I was really disturbed by the decisions I was making because, again, it was that double life."

The more time she spent with Brent, the less she helped with the youth group at church. The teens called her, asking why she wasn't there. She couldn't be. Depression settled in.

She decided to return to the last place where she felt she had solid grounding. She'd go back to the Ranch. Unaware of her current lifestyle choices, the ministry staff accepted her application as an intern.

But this time she was determined. God would have her whole heart.

The concept of love is confusing, often misunderstood. It's definitely a word thrown around loosely. With the teens and young adults you know, get a conversation going that's centered around what love is in the context of true intimacy.

Even when we know a lot about sex—what leads us to get involved with it, and even why we should wait—we can still struggle with understanding some important things. One is that, like Suzy, we might make the choice to go back to it again, even when we know it's not the right time. Aaron Chidester, Garth Heckman, and Barbara Wilson—all of whom speak to teens and young adults about waiting for God's timing for sex—have some great insights.

"Sex is an amazing, powerful thing, and it's safe within the proper boundaries," Aaron says. He talks about the progression in physical intimacy: "Relationships begin by holding hands and, step by step, progress to having intercourse." This will naturally happen even when two people follow the proper boundaries of dating and marriage given by God. So it's important to identify how to get there the right way, so you can set the right standards and boundaries, he says.

In talking about that progression, Garth refers to a theory he calls "the law of diminishing returns. . . . When you touch the hand of someone of the opposite sex, there's this sexual attraction—an explosion of chemicals. Then it dies down. And it's an addiction, so your brain wants a little more and a little more and a little more. It changes your brain like a piece of clay." Take it to the extreme—and then break off a sexually active relationship—and those chemicals will keep doing their stuff for quite some time, he says. That person, "over time, is no longer looking for another date. We always say you're looking for a dealer. You're looking for someone else to give you that next high."

Barbara says those same chemicals make us feel "good, special, in love, intensely bonded, and close—in fact closer than we really are emotionally." The cycle easily repeats and escalates into more sexual compromises. She says that the next time, "We'll initiate sex even sooner because we've already opened that pathway. We are more easily aroused sexually and know what that feels like, so we'll respond quicker to sexual stimuli."

Suzy knew God's grace. She was fully aware of the emptiness of a promiscuous lifestyle. And yet she didn't define her sex with Brent as being part of those old patterns. In her mind, this was a real relationship. She didn't go into it thinking it would involve sex, but different emotions and feelings stirred in her. She genuinely wanted love. With emotions came passions—and then wasn't sex expected? Another part of the picture was that Suzy had, as Barbara Wilson puts it, already opened that pathway.

Barbara adds, "If we would learn to build relationships without sex, the closeness we are craving would be met without needing the sex. Sex is really all about intimacy, but what we're usually seeking is emotional intimacy—someone who loves us and accepts us for who we are, not for what we can offer or do for them."

Sex has a powerful effect on us physically, emotionally, and spiritually. God knows that. That's why he designed it to be a love and intimacy shared between two people for life. A true intimacy.

Suzy would soon discover that kind of intimacy—what she had hoped for all along.

It's a pretty common belief that the earliest stages of intimacy are innocent ones, and "safe," but the truth is that one thing can quickly lead to another. Talk about this with the young people you're leading. Discuss healthy ways to respond to different situations.

HAVE A PLAN

Any of us could be like Suzy—not realizing how much of a hold our old lifestyle or destructive ways of thinking about ourselves has on our choices. We might allow a situation or encourage a scenario that leads to an intimacy that is entirely apart from God's plan and timing.

The thing is, while we're learning and growing deeper in understanding God's amazing plan for us, it's certain we will be in relationships—at least friendships—with the opposite sex. How do we keep those on track?

Proverbs 16:3 says, "Commit to the Lord whatever you do, and your plans will succeed." The first part of that verse tells us to commit whatever we're doing to the Lord. Keep him involved in our choices. Then our plans will go well—including in the area of our relationships.

But making sure we *have* a plan is a great idea too. So what are some things you can plan to do while hanging out with guys and girls that will keep your mind in the right place?

Here are a few ideas:

Commit to always hanging out in groups.

Avoid situations of close contact—like sitting on a couch in each other's arms, watching movies.

When you start dating, make sure each of you has an accountability partner—a mature person who is a good role model.

Focus on developing your character and getting to know lots of other guys and girls by serving together in your church or community.

Plan ahead for what you will do if you find yourself alone and in a risky situation with someone of the opposite sex.

Watch your conversations. Keep them clean. Keep them respectful.

Hang out with others who are committed to waiting for true intimacy. Share ideas on how to enjoy getting to know each other while helping your relationships stay healthy.

The idea is to enjoy real friendships now, without sex in the picture. It isn't because sex is dirty, but because it's something beautiful in its right time. You can look forward to it, but for now commit all you do to the Lord as you focus on protecting and preparing your heart.

*God, sex really is more powerful than I can handle
on my own. Please help me be aware of situations
that I should avoid. Show me where I am vulnerable.
If there is anything I'm not aware of that's hanging
on from my past, show me so I can bring it to you.
Strengthen me and help me see how I can make
purposeful plans to enjoy friendships without
compromising your timing and design for sex.* AMEN.

**Do not conform any longer to the pattern of this world,
but be transformed by the renewing of your mind.
Then you will be able to test and approve what
God's will is—his good, pleasing and perfect will.**

ROMANS 12:2

GOING DEEPER

Consider any ways that sex, or temptations to have sex,
might have a hold on you—ways you might gravitate toward,
even in your thoughts. What Scriptures can you begin to
memorize to help you in those moments?

■ In thinking about your relationships and avoiding sexual situations, how will you commit your way to the Lord (Proverbs 16:3) by making plans that honor him?

■ With others, or on your own, come up with a list of activities that would fit your situation and help you and your friends stay on track with relationships that honor God. What can you start doing right away?

DEEPER STILL

Any experience of sexual activity or sexual stimulus sticks in our minds, hangs on tenaciously, and won't go away without a fight. Consider your exposure and how that might have a hold on you. Pray and ask for God's forgiveness and strength. Ask him to renew your mind (Romans 12:2) and determine to move on.

Find a group or accountability person to help you keep steady. Share your commitment to accountability with that person, or a friend in that group.

thirteen

fourteen

I knew, after everything I had experienced,
God could still provide someone with purity and godly passion.
I longed for it—but I was scared to hope for it.

SUZY HELD BRENT'S LETTER in her shaking hands—his bitter response after she had called him and ended their relationship on Thanksgiving Day. Though it hurt, she wasn't surprised. In August she had moved back to the Ranch to work as an intern. She'd left without explaining why. She didn't know how to. She just knew she needed to put distance between the two of them so she could get back on track.

> **His angry words ripped through her.**
> **He said he felt used. He had told her he'd**
> **only have sex with the one he'd marry.**

Then she realized there was no way she could go back to seeing him.

His angry words ripped through her. He said he felt used. He had told her he'd only have sex with the one he'd marry, and she took advantage of him when he was grieving. How could she end their relationship?

She had to end it. None of her actions had been right. She had to make a new start.

In the next days, weeks, and months, she grieved her choices and prayed for God's forgiveness. While reading the Bible, she found a verse in Isaiah: "For your Maker is your husband—the Lord Almighty is his name—the Holy One of Israel is your Redeemer; he is called the God of all the earth" (Isaiah 54:5). God would be her husband for a while, the one who knew her deepest needs. Most of all, she hoped for his cleansing.

The days passed as she worked with the teens at the Ranch. She grew closer to God and was thankful for a time of not dating, or even being interested in, anyone. She'd wait until she understood better the potential depth of a God-honoring relationship.

Then Shane came to the Ranch as an intern. Other guys had come and gone, but this one was . . . interesting. Still, she remained cautious. It had been nine months since she had broken off the relationship with Brent. Was she ready?

"It will be five or ten years before I start dating again," she told him one day as they rode together on an errand for the staff.

Shane looked over at her as he maneuvered the Ranch truck down a country road. "Why that long?"

She shrugged. She wasn't sure how long she'd wait. She didn't want to blow it again. But then Shane was . . . amazing—someone who obviously loved God and cared deeply about the people around him. Her mind felt conflicted as her heart skipped.

    SEDUCED BY SEX : SAVED BY LOVE

Weeks passed. She grew more comfortable with the possibility of a relationship, and she and Shane began to spend their days off together. She felt his patience as he let her take the time she needed to figure things out. He respected her. She could feel that.

On one of their days off, they walked the shop-lined streets of an historic town fifteen miles up the highway from the Ranch. They talked about their lives growing up, about things they enjoyed, about situations with the teens at the Ranch. They stepped in and out of shops, enjoying the day, enjoying one another, then slowly headed back to Shane's truck.

Weeks passed. She grew more comfortable with the possibility of a relationship, and she and Shane began to spend their days off together. She felt his patience.

"Is it OK if I hold your hand?" he asked her.

She smiled. "Yes."

Shane took her hand. It felt so innocent but also intensely wonderful—like no one had ever touched her hand before. Was God making things new for her? She wanted to guard that innocence.

"Do you mind if I hold your hand *any* time?"

She thought for a moment and realized that, for now, she desperately needed the choice—for herself and for him. "No. I'd like you to ask."

"OK, no problem."

fourteen

She could tell he meant it. It really was fine.

Shane faced her, his look intense. "OK, how many is that?"
They had been dating for several months. He had finished his internship at the Ranch while she continued into her second year of service there, and he visited a couple weekends each month. They often spent their time walking and talking with each other. A favorite place was in a garden just a few miles from the ministry. The uncrowded walkways, including a quiet creek and statues depicting scenes from the Bible, felt restful.

She often used that time to tell him more of her past. This latest revelation—about more guys she had slept with—hit him hard.

They followed the path through the garden, still wet from a recent spring rain, and crossed a bridge that passed a waterfall, a place where they often stopped for conversation. This time, they kept walking the loop through the garden.

> She often used that time to tell him more of her past. This latest revelation—about more guys she had slept with—hit him hard.

She could feel the tension in his hand that held hers. Would this be the end of their relationship? But she knew she had to tell him everything. She glanced at Shane's face. His story was so different. He'd considered sex an intimacy he wanted to share one day only with his wife. For him to hear what she had chosen seemed to crush him each time she told him a little more. Then she would watch him leave on Sunday afternoons, knowing his drive home would be difficult as he wrestled through what she'd told him that weekend. So far, he always returned willing to continue their relationship. This time, though—maybe it was too much.

> **They sat down on a bench.**
> **The trees seemed to press in, and she felt**
> **sobs begin to rise from deep inside.**
> **She tried to choke them down.**

He finally spoke. "I thought it was just one guy, maybe two at the most. Now you're telling me there were more?" He seemed desperate to comprehend what she'd said.

They sat down on a bench. The trees seemed to press in, and she felt sobs begin to rise from deep inside. She tried to choke them down only to feel tears push their way out and wash down her cheeks. She waited for his response.

"I need to think about this," Shane said. He stared at the ground, but she could see in his expression the silent storm he fought inside. He shook his head. "I mean, it doesn't change what I feel about you, but I definitely need to process it."

Though she knew God had forgiven her again and again, she understood why Shane struggled. Why he may not be able to accept her. Before she even knew him, she had betrayed him. Now the painful path she'd chosen was breaking his heart. Sorrow and regret gripped her.

"I'm so sorry."

fourteen

He asked her for names, for dates.

Her sobs came hard as she poured out all the details that were necessary.

He wanted to know it all so there were no more surprises. Were there more guys she had slept with? Was she going to settle on a number of times she had had sex; would there be a point when it was all out? Why had she waited so long to tell him? Shane rocked forward and put his head in his hands. "I'm going to have to work this through. There are men that know you in a way I don't think anyone should, except me."

Then they were quiet, and though the sun shone through the trees, a sadness hung between them. She was thankful no one else walked by. They needed to be alone.

Shane lifted his head and she followed his gaze. Up the hill from them stood a life-size representation of Jesus hanging on a cross.

> Then they were quiet, and though the sun shone through the trees, a sadness hung between them.

Finally he spoke. "There's the cross. So it shouldn't matter to me." Then he met her eyes, laced his fingers with hers, and pointed to a small wooden sign in front of them. It read: "It is finished."

It is finished—words Jesus said at the cross as he took everyone's sins upon himself and died for them. Despite the pain of this moment, Suzy felt the completeness of that sacrificing

SEDUCED BY SEX : SAVED BY LOVE

love of Jesus. Shane knew it too. At that moment, he was able to give to her all of what Jesus had given him.

She looked into his eyes—so full of hurt, but also of love. They stayed there for some time, sitting quietly. She knew he'd still have that difficult drive home, but she felt his forgiveness. Knowing the worst about her, he would come back.

Finally, Shane stood and pulled her to her feet. Without words they walked to his truck. As they left the path, she detected the scent of the recent spring rain, the smell of a garden freshly washed.

> **Let us acknowledge the Lord; let us press on to acknowledge him. As surely as the sun rises, he will appear; he will come to us like the winter rains, like the spring rains that water the earth.**
>
> HOSEA 6:3

MY HOSEA

Suzy had experienced the destruction of false intimacy, its distortions and traps. She had walked its paths of lies that sucked the life out of her. After she thought she had wrestled free, she felt its tendrils pull her back.

And then finally—freedom.

God had shown her his plan for her life, and she saw it and acknowledged it. She pushed forward to a place where she fully entrusted to him her life and her dreams for love. And then she discovered God's plans included Suzy and Shane . . . together.

fourteen

"He is my Hosea," she says of Shane today. She refers to an Old Testament prophet who took a prostitute (commonly called a "harlot" in that day) as his wife and loved her. The story is representative of God loving the unfaithful nation of Israel. For Suzy, her Hosea represents God forgiving her and bringing an amazing relationship with Shane in spite of all her unfaithfulness. Shane, who had every intention of one day marrying someone who, like he, had saved the sacred intimacy of sex for marriage. Shane, who instead knew that God had brought Suzy to him to be his wife. Her past mattered—definitely. It ripped through him. And he still loved her.

So you're wondering: Yes, Suzy and Shane did marry. And though Suzy at times continues to work through past regrets and wounds, she can confidently say today, "Shane is passionately loving me in a way that Christ would be proud to call him his son."

Today, even in the first moments of spending time with Suzy and Shane, you witness the love they have for each other. Shane said, "There have been huge obstacles and deep valleys because of the way Suzy's past affects her now, but when the only language you speak is hope and love, then there is no other way. It all comes back to Christ—it always does. We are beautiful because he loves us."

Suzy sees Shane as more than just someone God provided for her to live out the rest of her days with. She said, "He is my best friend, someone with unending patience, and someone who chooses to see the best in me. When I fail, he sends me flowers. He doesn't remind me where I've come from. He's amazing."

SEDUCED BY SEX : SAVED BY LOVE

They have a family now, with three kids—two girls, one boy, all under the age of five—and another on the way at the time this book was written. For them, it just adds to the love they can share together. Suzy said, "The fun lately is enjoying our kids: *Look what we made together and how beautiful they are, and how they are full of life.*"

Shane and Suzy's hearts are set toward being in ministry together. Shane hopes to attend a seminary and teach Bible classes in a church or on a college campus. Suzy wants to work with teens and young women and—anytime it may help—share her story.

Her journey took her down the painful paths of false intimacy, something she will always remember with some sadness and tears. But God, in his unrelenting pursuit of her heart, loved her, healed her, and redeemed her. He set her feet on a new path so she could discover the gift of true intimacy he had for her all along.

> Those who have traveled down painful paths of sexual compromise may find it difficult to believe that God would ever bring something good for them in the future. They may stop trying. Help them gain a sense of hope for an exciting future. Encourage them to dream and create steps for their goals.

Wherever you might be on your journey, God is somewhere near. If you haven't already, invite him to join the journey with you. He is the only one who can help you find the intimacy your heart longs for.

All of those who shared their stories for this book have taken their own journeys out of false intimacy. They've experienced God's healing and restoration, have reclaimed his design for true intimacy, and now look forward to God unfolding his plan in their lives.

Nicole continues to pray for God to heal her and mold her to be more like him. She's praying she will one day experience God's plan for marriage in the way he had in mind for her all along.

Ryan wants God to be the center of everything, especially in his relationships. He isn't sure how God plans to unfold his future, but he's sure that if it includes marriage, God will have someone wonderful for him and it will happen at the right time for both of them.

Christine looks forward to meeting her "amazing husband." She doesn't know who he is yet, but knows he'll be deeply devoted to Christ and that he will love and respect her for who she is and will lead their physical relationship in purity.

Jordan says that until he finds the woman he'll marry, he doesn't even want to go as far as holding another girl's hand. He plans, with God's help, to completely save himself for his wife.

Reese recently admitted to a young woman that he "didn't even consider waiting." It broke his heart to look into her eyes and say that, but he's now committed to God's standard and prays that God will guide their relationship.

Amanda and Kevin look forward to deepening their relationship with God and each other. Even though their marriage began with hurtful challenges and circumstances because of their compromises, they are enjoying the journey of getting to know each other on many levels of true intimacy.

Love stories. You can read another one in the Bible in the Song of Songs. The poetic narrative opens with a couple expressing their love for one another, and the story continues as they court, fall in love, marry, and fall more deeply in love. Their passion and enjoyment of one another grows until it is fully expressed in an intimate, sexual union within marriage.

Two becoming one. Sex, beautifully expressed and enjoyed within the safe boundaries of a relationship of lifelong commitment, respect, and trust. God's plan. His plan for you. Ask him to etch that on your heart and don't let anything or anyone stop you from fully claiming it for your future.

> My lover spoke and said to me,
> "Arise, my darling,
> my beautiful one, and come with me.
> See! The winter is past;
> the rains are over and gone."
> SONG OF SONGS 2:10, 11

God, here I am on my own journey. I need your strength in order to keep going in the right direction—toward you and all that you have for me in my relationships and my life. I see how so much is sacrificed in false intimacy, but that doesn't have to be a part of my future. Draw me close and deepen my commitment to you. Prepare me for a future of serving you and honoring you in every way, including how, in the way you designed, I may someday fully love and honor the one I am to marry. AMEN.

GOING DEEPER

■ God's grace and pursuing love are a huge part of Suzy's story. Consider how that same grace and love are a part of your journey.

■ False intimacy and true intimacy. When you consider the contrasts and consequences of each, and what you want for your life, how does that knowledge affect your choices for your future?

■ On any journey we may hit moments where we feel ripped off track. We lose hope, motivation, or our sense of the right direction. What can you plan to do now that will help you during these difficult times?

DEEPER STILL

Think and pray about your future. Begin a journal, write a poem or story, paint a picture, or create a collage—something that reflects what you're looking forward to in all that God has ahead for you.

A LETTER FROM SUZY

IN MY ONE CHANCE to write to you here, there are so many things I want to say. I want you to know I am praying for you. I want you to know that I know what it feels like to look at your own life, and despise what you see, to feel trapped in who you've become and the cycle of compromises you've made. Dear friend, I've made choices in my life where, I thought for sure, there was no turning back. The consequences were detrimental at best, and often I was left with gaping wounds in the depths of my soul.

What can I tell you that will make a difference? I can only pray God reaches through my story and touches your life for the better.

An important point for me to make is that you haven't gone where God will not go. He is in active pursuit of you. Sometimes we think we need to clean up our lives to come to him. Not so. If you are in the muck, turn around. He is there.

In the midst of all my facades, lies, promiscuity, self-destruction, and selfishness, the God of sinners pulled me to himself, set my feet on solid ground, wiped off the dirt, and began to make me whole. If he can do that for me, then he can do that—and even more, if needed—for you.

A LETTER FROM JAN

THIS BOOK WAS WRITTEN with you in mind. At first I struggled because sex is such a huge topic. How would I be sure I could cover everything you would want to know about it? I realized, very quickly, I couldn't.

So I prayed. I prayed for you. I prayed for this book. And in praying I felt that I might do many things with these pages as I told the stories of others and invited a dialogue about sex. But I *had* to do one thing for sure: Go for the heart—your heart.

After all, it's your heart that makes the difference in what you choose to do with anything you read or consider about sex.

So above anything you might or might not fully grasp about sex, may you know God's pursuit of you and may you keep your heart fully open to him. I'm convinced that if you do these things, you'll have no room for false intimacy. You'll discover healing for those wounds and the confusing perceptions that send you there. You'll know in an instant when you're walking the thin line of compromise.

And you'll be attuned to his voice, the one that calls you back into the safety of his boundaries, back to his design for intimacy. True intimacy, not a false one.

I wish for you the most amazing love story you could ever imagine.

RESOURCES

The Web

WWW.CHOOSE2LIVEFREE.COM is a Christian site for teens and young adults. The site includes resources and links for lots of issues, including information and encouragement for staying on track with God's design for sex. Also addressed is self-injury. Visit frequently and join others in keeping inspired to *live free.*

WWW.BARBARAWILSON.ORG is Barbara's site, where you can read about her book, *The Invisible Bond,* and view issues of her *Pure Impact* newsletter.

WWW.BWUNITED.COM is where you'll find information on Garth Heckman and Phil Okongo-Gwoke's many programs for schools, including abstinence. Both men also are speakers for Great to Wait Rallies. See WWW.GREATTOWAIT.COM.

Books

Scars That Wound : Scars That Heal—A Journey Out of Self-Injury— If part of your story involves self-injury, as with Suzy, this book delves deeply into that topic. It includes Jackie's journey out of self-harm, the stories of many others, and helpful information and resources.
Jan Kern, Standard Publishing, 2007

The Invisible Bond: How to Break Free from Your Sexual Past—The author has experienced the challenges of a troubled sexual past and learned how to be set free. This is an excellent book that discusses how bonding occurs in the body, soul, and mind. It blends scientific research with Scripture and includes a practical study guide to help readers experience their own freedom.
Barbara Wilson, Multnomah Publishers, 2006

Sex Has a Price Tag: Discussions about Sexuality, Spirituality, and Self Respect—The authors speak honestly in this book for guys and girls about sex and dating. Included are commonsense warnings about, and consequences of, sex outside of God's boundaries, along with biblical examples and dating alternatives.
Pam Stenzel with Crystal Kirgiss, Youth Specialties, 2003

And the Bride Wore White: Seven Secrets to Sexual Purity—The author tells her personal story, including excerpts from her own journals, to share the challenges of temptations in dating. She lists seven secrets for applying sexual purity to a young woman's life.
Dannah Gresh, Moody Publishers, 2004

COLIN WAS LOOKING FOR
AN EASY WAY TO ESCAPE REALITY. . .

But it wasn't long before he found himself
trapped by Internet obsession. Follow his real-
life story from loneliness, to isolation, to friendship
in the third book in the Live Free series—

EYES ONLINE : EYES ON LIFE

A LIVE FREE BOOK

Available fall 2008.

Visit **www.standardpub.com**
or your local bookstore.

one

I felt like the Internet was where I belonged.

COLIN LEANED FORWARD IN HIS CHAIR. The soft creak didn't register, but then neither did the songs playing through his iPod. The images and words on his computer monitor drew his full attention.

Another shooting at a school, this time on a college campus.

Though far away, this one was more devastating than others he'd heard about. He shook his head, studied the monitor. *How did it happen?*

Colin clicked and followed links to page after page and took in more details of the story. Finally, he drew in a breath and sat back in his chair. Still staring at the screen, he slid his desk drawer open and popped out a quirky ball that fit in the palm of his hand. Colin's hands were never still for long. As he pounded the ball from one palm to the other, a red light pulsed from the center of the open, twisted bands of rubber.

What set the guy off? Didn't anyone see this coming? Could it have been prevented?

More questions pulsed through his mind. Emotions flashed. Anger one moment, sadness the next. Tears burned. He coughed and swallowed.

Colin dropped the ball back into the drawer. A final red blink flickered as he slid the drawer shut. He set an elbow on the desk, leaned his chin into his hand, and with the other hand clicked on a new link.

Some of the victims had run and hid. Some played dead. The stories were conflicted regarding details like how many were shot and how many had died, but there were a lot. Even though thousands of miles away, it seemed starkly real—not like some video game people could walk away from.

Colin shuddered. He reached up, pushed his glasses up his nose, and adjusted one of his earphones. As the final notes of a Relient K song faded into a Switchfoot mix, he dropped his hand back to the computer keyboard. He favored using keyboard shortcuts over the mouse.

In the quietness of the pause between songs, voices buzzed from another room, shifting his attention. He pulled his earphones off and the wires dropped around his neck. He heard the phone ring, someone answering. He picked up a pen from his desk and twirled it over his thumb and through his fingers. As he did, he nodded his head along with the beat of a drumming rhythm he made with his tongue. The sounds around him grew quiet. He looked back at the screen.

What had he been doing? *Oh yeah, the story . . .*

Maybe he'd create a tribute to the victims. A video scenario ran through his mind. He imagined designing the video, accompanying it with a song he'd play on the piano and sing.

He tossed the pen on his desk and reread the story on the monitor. A couple more clicks and a link showed a picture of the alleged shooter's face. Colin felt the anger rise again. *Man, how could he do it?* He shook his head and sat back. The eyes of the shooter seemed to stare into his. Then it hit him. The injured and killed weren't the only victims. The guy who shot them was a victim too. A person. Someone he could have known.

Colin swallowed. Could he ever have gotten so desperate,

angry, or hurting to do what this guy did—gone off and shot people? Colin shook his head in answer to his own question. But . . . he sure could understand him in a lot of ways. If he were there, walking the hallways with the guy, seeing him on the streets, he would have recognized the signs—the confusion and fear in his eyes, the raw loneliness.

The thought sucked him back to a time—not too distant—of his own loneliness. He had felt it for years, like a menacing shadow he couldn't shake. The taunting when he was younger, the uncomfortable feelings of being left out, some of it by his own choice. The kids at his elementary school talking about something sexual or trying to be cool by being disrespectful to teachers or bullying other kids. He hadn't wanted to be part of that. Sometimes he found himself in the middle of it only because he happened to be the one they were targeting.

Then, in junior high, he'd joined in on some of it just to fit in. Or at least to be left alone. The loneliness still followed him from one year to the next, right into high school. He had felt it everywhere—at church, sometimes even at home. But school, that was the worst. He showed up every day and would rather have been anywhere else. Sure, at lunch he hung out with a few friends he knew from band, sometimes laughing and cracking jokes. Mostly he just got through those days, avoiding as much interaction as possible.

Still, there was Lisa. She was nice. They were friends, hanging out during band period and band events. They talked. Sometimes, as friends, they held hands or hugged. Then, one day, even that friendship was threatened, and he became the target of bullying again. He remembered it well. He was walking between some buildings on campus. The sun's heat pierced his T-shirt. Just as a bell rang for class, he felt an arm come across his shoulder. Two guys closed in and flanked him while he walked. Big guys—bigger than he was, anyway. One he'd known from earth science class.

"You've been hanging out a lot with Lisa," that one had said. The other guy added, "Yeah, I don't want to see you hanging around my girlfriend anymore." He'd pegged them as mostly talk, but still able to inflict damage if they wanted. Their purpose was to intimidate, and they had accomplished it big time. As they walked away, his heart beat hard in his chest. He remembered the sickening dread that spread like thick goo in his stomach. It stayed with him through the last couple of class periods that day.

When he got home, he'd skipped his usual routine of grabbing something to eat or drink. He headed straight for his room, dropped off his stuff on his bed, and slid into his chair in front of his computer. He sat there, legs stretched, one foot tapping. His heartbeat had calmed, but he couldn't shake the feeling that clung in his stomach. He scooted his chair toward the monitor and got online.

The great escape. And he knew it would work.

Colin picked up the pen again, tapping it on his knee as his thoughts slid back to the college shooter's face. Maybe the guy had tried to escape too—from fears, loneliness, something. He only needed one good friend. Just one. Someone to tell him he mattered. Someone to listen.

Maybe I could have been that friend.

The video tribute still formed in Colin's thoughts and played through his mind. *Someone to listen.* Would the guy have been willing to talk about what was going on inside? Could lives have been saved? Maybe. Maybe not.

Loneliness. Not a good thing. Not a good thing at all.

Again Colin's thoughts took him back to the day those guys threatened him.

It had felt natural to turn to the Internet to shake what happened. It was where he spent most of his time—especially by the time he was in high school . . .

Even in the afternoon his bedroom remained mostly dark, except for the glow from the monitor. Lights were off. Blinds were drawn closed. As Colin sat at his computer, he could almost feel the guy's arm across his shoulder, still pressing down. Leave his girlfriend alone? . . . He didn't even *know* Lisa had a boyfriend—at least not one that serious.

Lisa was one of the few good things about school. When they were talking and laughing together he could forget how lonely other times of the day or week were.

That day his online activities started simply, innocently. He opened his e-mail, checked his inbox, and read a couple of messages. He clicked on video game bulletin boards and joined a web chat about codes and the latest hot video games. While he read those, he IM'd several friends he'd gotten to know online. Maybe he'd tell one of them what happened that day.

The afternoon hours pushed toward dinnertime as he moved from chatting into a game of RuneScape. His avatar teleporting across the realm of Gielinor reflected in his glasses.

With eyes and mind completely focused, he maneuvered through the fantasy kingdoms fighting monsters and completing quests. With the background sounds of music and seagulls screeching, he was pulled into a world far away from the guys who had threatened him, far from the uncomfortable realm of the high school halls and passageways.

Food smells coming from the kitchen made his stomach growl. He ignored it.

"Come eat some dinner," his dad said as he passed Colin's room.

"OK, Dad." Colin shifted and clicked his mouse a few more times to fight off a monster, got to a safe part of an island, and closed the game. He pushed away from his computer. As he stepped out into the hallway and the lighted living room, he blinked a few times to adjust to the brightness. Dad was sitting in front of the TV, already eating.

"I made spaghetti and a salad," Mom said. She was standing at the kitchen counter blending a meal shake for Chris, Colin's older brother, who had mental retardation. Mealtimes were a challenge for Mom, so they often ate wherever, instead of at the dining room table.

"Thanks, Mom. I'll just have a hot dog."

"OK. There's plenty if you change your mind."

"Yeah, I know. Thanks for making dinner. I'm just not that hungry." He kept his choices to a few favorites. He knew she wouldn't press the issue.

Colin warmed his hot dog and bun in the microwave, wrapped it in a paper towel, and headed back to his room. He didn't want to join Dad in watching TV tonight. The day's events too easily pushed into his mind again and got him down.

He'd avoid that any way he could. He bit into his hot dog as he settled back into his desk chair.

Outside it had grown darker. The monitor's soft light cast a glow across his room. Colin took a few more bites and used his free hand to check e-mail and message boards again. As he popped in the last bite, he wiped his hand on his jeans and opened up RuneScape to resume his game. His thoughts about the day grew more distant, as if he were walling them up in some forgotten corridor. Not a place he planned to return to—if possible, ever.

A couple of hours passed quickly. Sounds coming from the other rooms and passing down the hall told Colin that Chris, and then Mom and Dad, were heading to bed. Mom and Dad poked their heads in at different times to say goodnight.

"Don't stay up too late, Colin," Mom said.

"Yeah, OK." Colin nodded a goodnight.

After a little more time passed, Colin checked the quietness of the house. Everyone was asleep by now. He listened again, to be sure. Then he turned to other Internet activities he felt might ease the unrest of the day and his loneliness.

A few clicks and . . . he was trapped. Jaws clamping down, deceptive and seductive, drawing Colin in deeper and deeper.

> As I sink in despair, my spirit ebbing away,
> you know how I'm feeling,
> Know the danger I'm in,
> the traps hidden in my path.
> PSALM 142:3 (THE MESSAGE)